In Defense of Rights: Attacks on Lawyers and Judges in 1993

Lawyers Committee for Human Rights
330 Seventh Avenue
New York, NY 10001
Tel: (212)629-6170; Fax: (212)967-0916

Washington Office:
100 Maryland Avenue, NE
Washington, DC 20002
Tel: (202) 547-5692; Fax: (202)543-5999

Printed in the United States of America

Lawyers Committee for Human Rights

Since 1978 the Lawyers Committee for Human Rights has worked to promote international human rights and refugee law and legal procedures in the United States and abroad. The Chairman of the Lawyers Committee is Marvin E. Frankel; Michael H. Posner is its Executive Director. George Black is Research and Editorial Director.

Copies of this report are available from:

Lawyers Committee for Human Rights
330 Seventh Avenue, 10th Floor
New York, New York 10001 USA

ISBN: 0-934143-67-6

FRANCOIS GUY MALARY
1943-1993

TABLE OF CONTENTS

BY R. WILLIAM IDE III
PRESIDENT, AMERICAN BAR ASSOCIATION

For five years now, the Lawyers Committee for Human Rights has published *In Defense of Rights*, an annual report of attacks against lawyers and judges worldwide. It has now become something of a tradition for the Lawyers Committee to release this report on May 1 each year. It is on this date that the American Bar Association annually celebrates Law Day USA. The purpose of Law Day is to reserve a "special day of celebration by the American people in appreciation of their liberties and to provide an occasion for rededication to the ideals of equality and justice under laws." Law Day has also become an occasion to honor those around the world who are engaged in the democratic struggle for justice. For those of us in the American legal profession, this means above all the colleagues and counterparts whose struggles are documented in this volume.

The men and women who appear in the pages of *In Defense of Rights* understand better than anyone that the ability of lawyers and judges to work freely and independently is a cornerstone of any society that claims to respect human rights and the rule of law. In their refusal to back down in the face of violent attack, threats and harassment, they remind us of forcefully of our own obligation to advance, nurture and protect the rule of law worldwide. The 1993 edition of *In Defense of Rights* documents 266 cases, affecting some 415 individual lawyers and judges as well as 16 groups and legal institutions.

Those of us who thought that the end of the Cold War would usher in a new era of respect for human rights has been rudely disappointed by recent events. For decades, it was easy to see human rights abuses as a function of a global ideological struggle. Today, that narrow mold has been broken, and the sources of abuse are multiple and confusing. Abuses may arise from ethnic hostilities, from conflicts between secular regimes and religious fundamentalists, and, in some countries, from the basic breakdown of any functional legal system.

Lawyers and judges in many nations of the world must often work at considerable risk to their lives. No fewer than 30 legal professionals were killed in the line of duty in 1993. Eight were murdered in Algeria alone, presumably by Islamist militants; eight more died in Colombia at the violent intersections of drug trafficking, paramilitary activity and counterinsurgency. If anyone thought that celebrity and international connections offered effective protection, the murder of Haitian Justice Minister Guy Malary surely proved that no one is immune from attack.

In addition to these individual attacks, however, governments and others now increasingly target institutions that are the citizen's first line of defense against human rights abuses. In some instances, this means the organized bar and judiciary. In Argentina, for instance, the entire Buenos Aires provincial judiciary received death threats, to the point where judges no longer bothered to report them to the authorities. In Turkey, Peru and elsewhere, the right of legal defense in politically unpopular cases has all but vanished under the assault of anti-terrorism laws that identify lawyers with the political views of their clients. Also under attack are the non-governmental human rights advocacy groups that have mushroomed throughout the world in the last decade. In these groups, lawyers are invariably the prime movers. During the aborted transition to civilian rule, lawyers with Nigeria's Civil Liberties Organization have been repeatedly arrested and harassed. Saudi Arabia's first ever human rights group, the Committee for the Defense of Legitimate Rights, was shut down just ten days after its founding; its lawyer-leaders were jailed, fired or had their licenses suspended.

The birth of groups like these, and the growing international network of those interested in their work, underscores the fact that the promotion and protection of the rule of law can no longer be a parochial concern. The American Bar Association is an active participant in this process. Since 1975, when the ABA House of Delegates adopted a "Rule of Law" resolution recognizing the worldwide need for an independent legal profession and judiciary, ABA presidents have written to foreign heads of state requesting information and expressing concern in specific cases. Each of these cases has involved allegations of harassment or persecution against a lawyer or judge. In this effort, the monthly appeals of the Lawyers Committee's Lawyer-to-Lawyer Network are an invaluable source of information. Similar procedures are followed by national bar groups in other countries, as well as by a number of state and local bar associations in the United States. The ABA actively supports these initiatives, and encourages those bars not already engaged to consider adopting their own "rule of law" resolutions and procedures for responding to such cases. These initiatives, in turn, are reinforced by the work of regional and international bar groups, such as the International Bar Association, the *Union Internationale des Avocats*, the Inter-American Bar Association, the African Bar Association, the Arab Lawyers Union and LAWASIA. As we commemorate Law Day 1994, let us pledge to redouble our commitment to our beleaguered colleagues worldwide. Individually and collectively, our efforts *can* make a difference.

Chicago, Illinois
May 1994

Preface and Acknowledgments

This is the fifth annual edition of *In Defense of Rights*. The 1993 edition includes data on 266 cases in 49 countries, affecting 415 individual judges and lawyers and 16 legal institutions and advocacy groups.

Although these figures give some sense of the alarming scale of abuse against the legal profession, *In Defense of Rights* does not pretend to be an encyclopedia. We know that there are many abuses that never come to the attention of outside observers; dozens of other cases have been excluded from these pages because they come to us only in fragmentary form or in accounts that cannot be independently corroborated. For a case to be included in this book often requires extensive and painstaking research, and wherever possible detailed information from at least two reliable sources. This is a complex exercise, involving a pyramid of groups and individuals from around the world.

There are at least four layers to this pyramid. The Lawyers Committee's research for *In Defense of Rights* is directed by the coordinators of our international human rights program, each with his or her own specialized regional knowledge. Under their supervision, a team of legal interns compiles data on possible cases with the help of a network of volunteers and consultants — many of whom also assist other Lawyers Committee projects, such as our Freedom of Association project or our annual *Critique* of the State Department's human rights reporting. These interns, volunteers and consultants, in turn, are in regular touch with a network of hundreds of local human rights groups, individual advocates and non-governmental organizations with access to the facts on the ground. It is these groups and individuals — our colleagues as well as our sources — who give life and breath to the international human rights movement.

Given the scale of this effort, it is incumbent on us to thank a large number of people and organizations for their efforts on behalf of this project. We express our gratitude, first of all, to a number of other international legal and human rights organizations. These include: The American Association for the Advancement of Science; the American Bar Association; both the International Secretariat and the U.S. Section of Amnesty International; the Andean Commission of Jurists (Colombian and Peruvian Sections); Article 19; the Committee to Protect Journalists (CPJ); the *Fédération Internationale des Ligues des Droits de l'Homme*; Freedom House; Human Rights Watch; the International Commission of Jurists in Geneva, and especially its Centre for the Independence of Judges and Lawyers (CIJL), whose invaluable annual report, *Attacks Against Justice*, is in many ways a companion publication to this one; the International Human Rights Law Group; International PEN and its Writers in Prison Committee; InterRights; the Law Society of England and Wales; Minnesota Advocates for Human Rights; *Stichting Advocaten voor Advocaten* (Netherlands); and the World Organization Against Torture. We are also grateful to a number of individual country desk officers and embassy personnel of the U.S. Department of State.

For our research on Africa, we are indebted to: Adam Abdelmoula, the Centre for the Victims of Violence and Torture (South Africa), the Civil Liberties Committee (Malawi), the Civil Liberties Organization (Nigeria), the Committee in Defense of Human Rights (Nigeria), the Constitutional Rights Project (Nigeria), Nomsa Daniels, Ahmadou Gueye, the Legal Resources Centre (South Africa), Matadi Nenga of the Kinshasa Bar Association, John Matthew, Helet Merkling, Mlaba Makhaye and Partners (Durban, South Africa), Richard Molewa, Mordecai Msisha of the Malawi Law Society, the National Association of Democratic Lawyers (Nigeria), Ngefa Atondoko Guillaume, the Nigerian Bar Association, Salua Nour,

Festus Okoye, Peter Rosenblum, the Sudan Human Rights Organization, Mary Caroline Yates and the Zaire Human Rights Association.

In Asia: Mubasher Ahmad, the Burma Information Group, *Burma Issues*, *Burma Monitor*, *Burma Review*, the Burmese Relief Center, Mark Cammack, Claudia D'Andrea, the Free Legal Assistance Group (FLAG) (Philippines), the Human Rights Commission of Pakistan, Human Rights in China (New York), INFORM (Sri Lanka), the International Human Rights Group of Punjab, the International NGO Forum on Indonesian Development (The Hague), Margaret John, Lawyers for Democracy in Sri Lanka (London), Martin Lee, Stephen S. Lee, Lembaga Bantuan Hukum (LBH) (Indonesia), Mei Chin Cheng, Golpan Nair, Cecil Rajendra, Ridarsen Galingging, Francis T. Seow, Harinder Singh Sidhu, the South Asia Documentation Centre, Ting Yee Wang and Mujeeb Ur Rehman.

In Europe and the former Soviet Union: Professor Eva Brantley, British/Irish Rights Watch, the Council for the Defense of Human Rights and Freedoms in Prishtina (Kosovo), Martin Flaherty, Neymetullah Gunduz, the Human Rights Foundation of Turkey, the Istanbul Bar Association, the Kurdistan Human Rights Project, the Kurdistan Information Center, Abdumannob Pulatov, Yuri Shmidt, the Ukrainian Lawyers League and Lois Whitman.

In Latin America and the Caribbean: The *Academia Mexicana de Derechos Humanos*, *Alfalit Dominicano*, the *Asociación Colombiana de Juristas Demócratas*, the *Asociación Colombiana pro Derechos Humanos*, the *Asociación Guatemalteca de Juristas*, the *Asociación Nacional de Abogados Democráticos* (Mexico), the *Asociación para la Promoción Social Alternativa — MINGA* (Colombia), the *Asociación pro Derechos Humanos* (APRODEH) (Peru), *Asonal Judicial* (Colombia), the Bar Association of Trinidad and Tobago, Barrera, Siquieros y Torres Randa, S.C. (Mexico),

Jayme Benvenuto de Lima Jr., Rachel Biderman Furriela, Licda. Luisa Campos, Caribbean Rights/Caribbean Human Rights Network, Sandra Carvalho, the *Centro de Derechos Humanos Fray Bartolomé de las Casas* (Mexico), the *Centro de Derechos Humanos "Miguel A. Pro Juárez"* (PRO-DH) Mexico), the *Centro de Documentación de Honduras* (CEDOH), the *Centro Dominicano de Asesoría e Investigaciones Legales* (CEDAIL), the *Centro de Estudios Jurídicos e Investigación Social* (Bolivia), the *Centro de Investigación y Educación Popular* (CINEP) (Colombia), the *Centro de Investigaciones Sociales y Asesorías Legales Populares* (CISALP) (Argentina), Professor Paul Chevigny, the *Colectivo de Organizaciones Populares* (Dominican Republic), the *Colegio de Abogados* (Dominican Republic), the Colombian Human Rights Commission, the *Comisión de Derechos Humanos de Guatemala*, the *Comisión Ecuménica de Derechos Humanos* (Ecuador), the *Comisión de Solidaridad y Defensa de los Derechos Humanos, A.C.* (COSYDDHAC) (Mexico), the *Comité de Solidaridad con los Presos Políticos* (Colombia), the *Comité Dominicano de los Derechos Humanos*, the *Comité para la Defensa de los Derechos Humanos en Honduras*, (CODEH), the *Comité Regional para la Defensa de los Derechos Humanos* (Colombia), the *Consejero Presidencial para los Derechos Humanos* (Colombia), the *Consejo Regional Indígena del Cauca* (CRIC) (Colombia), the *Coordinadora Nacional de Derechos Humanos* (Peru), Maria Cristinia, the Cuban Committee for Human Rights, Wilson da Silva, Dr. José do Carmo Siekueira, Alicia Ely-Yamin, Dra. Rosa Fernández, the *Fundación Myrna Mack* (Guatemala), the Guatemalan Human Rights Commission/USA, Orlando Herrera, the Human Rights Institute of the *Universidad Centroamericana José Simeón Cañas* (IDHUCA) (El Salvador), the Human Rights Office of the Archbishopric of Guatemala, the *Instituto Apoio Juridico Popular* (AJOP) (Brazil), the *Instituto de Defensa*

Legal (Peru), the *Instituto de Estudios Jurídicos de El Salvador*, the *Instituto de Estudios Jurídicos de la Mujer* (Argentina), the *Instituto Latinoamericano de Servicios Legales Alternativos* (Colombia), the Inter-Church Committee on Human Rights in Latin America, María Teresa Jardí, *Juristas Mexicanos,* Carlos López de Belva, the National Coalition on Haitian Refugees, Sister Michael Mary Nolan, the Pan-American Committee of the Institute in the Service of Human Rights (Geneva), the Pastoral Land Commission (Brazil), Dr. Paulo Sérgio Pinheiro, the Platform of Haitian Organizations for the Defense of Human Rights, the *Procurador de los Derechos Humanos de Guatemala*, the *Programa Venezolano de la Educación en Derechos Humanos* (Venezuela), the Trinidad and Tobago Bureau on Human Rights, the United Nations Civilian Mission in Haiti (MICIVIH) and the Washington Office on Latin America (WOLA).

In the Middle East and North Africa: The Arab Association for Human Rights (Israel); the Arab Lawyers Union; the Arab Organization for Human Rights; the Committee for the Defense of Democratic Freedoms and Human Rights in Syria; Liberty for the Muslim World (UK); the Egyptian Organization for Human Rights; the Gaza Centre for Rights and Law; and *Al-Haq* (West Bank).

Interns involved in the research and production of *In Defense of Rights* were: Sherley Ayala, Laura Brooks, Sybil Chabane, Sharmila Desai, Lorenzo Dominguez, Jennifer Kerr, Sarah Lavine-Kass, Maggie Miqueo, Jessica Montell, Katherine Mulhern, Ani Oghali and Sheri Rosenberg. We owe special thanks to interns Betsy Jaffe and Shannon O'Neill, who set exemplary standards during their six months of full-time work on this project.

Volunteers and consultants on the project included: Elizabeth Barad, Nancy Batterman, Lauro M. Bueno, Rosario Conde-Johanek, Kay Eisenhower, K.S. Venkat Eswaran, Katherine Fleet, Patrick Gavigan, Timothy A. Gelatt, Evan Gottesman, Jeffrey Gracer, Pamela

Hoopes, Gordon Lai, Phil K. Lau, Scott Newton, D. Paul O'Brien, Anthony St.John, Raúl Sánchez, Elliot Schrage and Anne Stetson. In many of these cases, we are additionally grateful to the law firms that made it possible for these consultants to offer their pro bono services to the Lawyers Committee.

Members of the Lawyers Committee staff who assisted in the *In Defense of Rights* project were: Adotei Akwei, Joseph C. Eldridge, Neil Hicks, Mariana Katzarova, Jéneen M. Masih, Michael H. Posner, James D. Ross and Robert O. Weiner. We were fortunate to secure the energetic and expert assistance of Carol Conragan of the Vermont Law School for a crucial period of the research and production of this year's edition. Annette O'Donnell designed and typeset the text and oversaw production. The cover and artwork are by Pat Scully; the map was designed by Tom Sternal.

In Defense of Rights was coordinated and edited by George Black, Research and Editorial Director of the Lawyers Committee.

New York City
Lawyers Committee for Human Rights
May 1, 1994

Introduction

BY MARVIN E. FRANKEL
CHAIRMAN
LAWYERS COMMITTEE FOR HUMAN RIGHTS

To suggest to an American audience that the legal profession is a group in need of special protection may invite disbelief. Yet each year, this is precisely the argument that the Lawyers Committee advances through the pages of *In Defense of Rights*. Why lawyers and judges, surely one of the more privileged of social groups?

The easy answer is that we are a committee of lawyers, rooted in the profession, and that we therefore feel an obligation to report on the injustices and brutalities visited on our counterparts around the world. But there is also a more profound reason. Without security for those whose professional duty is to uphold and promote the rule of law, there can be no security for any citizen. There is no more accurate barometer of the general civic health of a society than the way it treats its legal professionals. In the United States, we are treated well; in dozens of countries around the world, our colleagues are treated deplorably.

The second argument grows more compelling each year as the rule of law is reduced, in one country after another, to the thinnest of lines protecting the population from unfettered executive power and generalized barbarity. Just three or four years ago, after the collapse of the Soviet Union and its satellites, it was fashionable to believe that the universal rule of liberal democracy had dawned. Only the technical details remained to be worked out. Today that optimism seems naive.

If anything is universal today, it is surely the threat to the rule of law. No form of government, and no ideology, has a monopoly on acts of violence and intimidation against lawyers and judges. The victims, too, cover the ideological spectrum; often, they are people whose understanding of their professional responsibilities has led them into the active promotion of human rights, frequently in alliance with a political cause. The Lawyers Committee takes no position on these matters and has never associated itself with any particular point of view. Our sole interest is that those who are lawfully engaged in the pursuit of the rule of law, impartially applied, are entitled to work in security and freedom.

There is a long roster of countries in which the legal profession faces fear and persecution. Some of the countries described in this book will appear obvious candidates for inclusion: few readers, for example, will be surprised to learn that Burma, Libya and Syria between them are holding 36 lawyers as longterm prisoners to punish them for their advocacy of basic human rights. By the same token, it will come as no surprise that legal professionals were victimized by war or civil conflict in Rwanda, Tajikistan or Zaire. Such countries may be considered, so to speak, "the usual suspects" of the human rights world.

But more dismaying is the fact that many countries that have supposedly embarked on — or even completed — the transition to democracy rank among the worst in offenses against laywers and human rights advocates. For example, by most criteria, Argentina and Guatemala are no longer seen as countries experiencing full-blown human rights emergencies. It is almost a decade now since these countries replaced their military rulers with elected civilians. But those who once wielded absolute power will fight jealously to hold the line against the encroaching tide of judicial professionalism and democratic accountability. In 1993, we reported 16 separate attacks on Guatemalan lawyers and judges, involving 37 individuals and two legal institutions. Many of the individuals targeted had sought, sometimes successfully, to hold military officers accountable for their crimes after decades of impunity. In Argentina, meanwhile, it is shocking to learn that *every single member* of the Buenos Aires provincial judiciary received death threats during 1993, to the point where judges ceased to bother reporting them to the authorities.

In situations like these, how is one to say clearly that the government is to blame? That, after all, has been the guiding principle of our Lawyer-to-Lawyer Network since its inception in 1987. The Network, and its monthly appeals on behalf of lawyers and judges at risk, remains the core of the *In Defense of Rights* project. In the letters that they write, Network participants — who now number more than 9,000 — hold offending governments accountable to internationally recognized human rights standards. For a case of abuse to be considered for inclusion as a Network appeal, there must be clear evidence of government culpability.

In Defense of Rights, however, has always gone a little further than this, and it may be in order to say a word about the criteria that we apply to the cases included in this volume. In many of the cases documented here, official action is direct and demonstrable — a lawyer is jailed by the state, tried on trumped-up charges, or executed by a government firing squad. But those who abuse lawyers do not often leave calling cards claiming responsibility for their deeds. Sometimes, government involvement cannot be clearly ascertained, but must be inferred from circumstantial evidence and from expert knowledge of established patterns of abuse in the country in question. At other times, governments are internally divided, and lawyers may be attacked, threatened or harassed by factional forces. In some cases we go on the principle that governments must be held responsible for the dereliction of their duty to guarantee the safety of their citizens, or their failure to conduct serious investigations of threats to the rule of law, even if these derive from non-governmental sources.

There are situations in which it is clear that the government itself bears no direct responsibility for the abuse, yet several such cases are included in these pages. In many countries, such as some in North Africa or in the Andean region of Latin America, the rule of law has effectively broken down. In such countries, state power is seriously contested and there is more than a single source of armed authority. Thus, we have chosen to list cases of judges and prosecutors murdered, presumably by militant Islamists, in Algeria. Similarly, we have included lawyers murdered in Colombia by rebel groups in areas where the government does not exercise effective control. But our criteria for including a case remain clear and consistent. In all cases, the motive for the abuse must be that it came as a consequence of the victim's pursuit of his or her professional duties.

In Defense of Rights does not claim to tell the whole story. We are aware, for example, of the murder of at least another 30 judges and lawyers in Colombia alone, but in circumstances that give no specific indication of the identity of the killers. We also know of at least five judges who have died in the ethnic civil war in Rwanda, but we have no further details of their deaths. Rwanda is one of a number of countries in which a combination of fear, poor communications and the relative absence of reliable local sources of information conspire to keep abuses from being known to the outside world.

Those circumstances are slowly being overcome, in one country after another. Information about rights violations has even begun to filter out of countries that we have traditionally considered to be closed. For the first time, *In Defense of Rights* has been able to document abuses of legal professionals in Saudi Arabia, one of the world's most suffocating absolutist regimes. The reason for this is straightforward: in 1993, Saudi Arabia saw the birth of its first non-governmental human rights organization, the Committee for the Defense of Legitimate Rights. Countries such as Saudi Arabia, Iraq or North Korea regard the human rights movement as a contagion, to be kept out at all costs. But it has begun to reach them, and there are now literally hundreds of human rights advocacy groups throughout the world. Many of them, such as the Saudi CDLR, are spearheaded by lawyers.

The Lawyers Committee for Human Rights feels a special affinity and responsibility toward these non-governmental advocacy groups. Their ability to operate freely is one of the best tests of whether the rule of law is operative, and of whether governments' promises of reform and democratization are sincere and effective. Groups like these are the focus of the Lawyers Committee's recently launched Freedom of Association Project. To these groups, and to the individual judges, lawyers, law students and law professors listed in these pages, we pledge our enduring support. Their work inspires us, and humbles us.

New York City
May 1, 1994

ISSUES OF CONCERN IN 1993

THE DEATH AND LEGACY OF GUY MALARY

Guy Malary, Justice Minister for the government of elected Haitian President Jean Bertrand Aristide, was ambushed and killed on October 14, 1993 outside his law office in the Haitian capital, Port-au-Prince. Although no suspects have been named or charged in connection with the murder, those familiar with the case believe either that the Haitian military and security forces were directly involved in the killing or that the culprits operated under their protection. According to bystanders at the scene of the crime, armed police and civilians intimidated witnesses and threatened to shoot news photographers immediately after the killing.

Mr. Malary, who was 50 when he died, left a successful private law practice when President Aristide tapped him in July 1993 to oversee planned reforms of the judicial system. Almost at once he began to receive repeated death threats from police auxiliaries (*attachés*). Despite the extreme risks to his personal safety, he became one of the first Aristide cabinet appointees to defy the threats and occupy his office.

Even as a government official, Guy Malary remained a reliable source of information on abuses against his fellow legal professionals for both the Lawyer-to-Lawyer Network and *In Defense of Rights*. Indeed, Mr. Malary's work, both in and out of government, incarnated the ideals behind these projects of the Lawyers Committee for Human Rights: preserving the role of advocates for basic rights and ensuring that the legal system is responsive to those who demand that it give meaning to those rights. To be sure, each person cited in this book pursued those goals. Rarely, however, has any one individual lawyer played such a role so critical that a nation's future hinged on his success or failure.

When the Lawyers Committee published its Lawyer-to-Lawyer Network Appeal on behalf of Guy Malary, immediately after his assassination, it requested members to write to President Bill Clinton, United Nations Secretary General Boutros Boutros-Ghali, and de facto leader of the Haitian military government, General Raoul Cédras. The fact that the Network sought for the first time to communicate with the leadership of the US government and the United Nations was a reflection not only of Mr. Malary's official position as a cabinet minister but rather of the international dimension of his efforts, and the degree of international responsibility for the chain of events that led up to his death.

By all accounts Guy Malary, who shunned partisan politics, did not seek his office. It sought him. The US government joined President Aristide in encouraging him to accept the nomination. Years earlier, Mr. Malary had worked with the Agency for International Development (AID) on a US-funded legal aid project that was subsequently terminated by the Duvalier government. It was then that he made a lasting impression on AID officials.

In 1993, the UN-brokered Governors Island Accord provided a blueprint for Haiti's transition back to constitutional rule that depended on the separation and reform of the police and military. AID and related agencies, together with international forces working under the auspices of the UN, designed programs for the police and army; AID also outlined plans for judicial reform initiatives. The planned reforms, and indeed a significant part of the entire transition process, depended on the passage of enabling legislation that was to be conceived and proposed by the Justice Ministry. For this reason, US officials were anxious for Mr. Malary, who was widely respected for his integrity and consensus building skills, to assume the crucial task of overseeing implementation of the reform effort.

As Minister of Justice, Guy Malary also oversaw another important legal effort — the investigation into the murder in mid-September of prominent Aristide supporter Antoine Izméry. Mr. Izméry had been dragged out of a church service and murdered in broad daylight by armed *attachés*. The brazenness of the execution epitomized the impunity of the military and its mirror twin, the institutional impotence of the judicial system. As Justice Minister, Mr. Malary knew that neither the system nor the planned reform would have any credibility without some response to a provocative killing that had been carried out in plain sight of international human rights monitors. He therefore pushed local prosecutors to investigate the crime, even as other Aristide-appointed ministry offices were barricaded or shut down by paramilitary supporters of the coup regime. As a result of these efforts, Mr. Malary had identified several suspects in the Izméry killing at the time of his own murder.

Guy Malary and others who were striving to return Haiti to civilian rule were aware of the risks entailed by their association with the efforts of the international community. However, these dangers were exacerbated by the failure of US and UN policy makers to adequately enforce the human rights provisions of the Governors Island Accord. For example, US-designed training programs to convert soldiers into police failed to include any provisions for sanctioning or removing human right violators from the security forces as a condition of US assistance.

Emboldened by this failure, and by additional signals that human rights concerns would be subordinate to other diplomatic imperatives, Haiti's military openly defied the international community, terrorizing the populace in a bid to retain control. Guy Malary's murder — taking place only two days after an angry mob had successfully turned away a ship carrying a contingent of US military trainers to Haiti — was widely viewed as a clear message to other officials not to get involved in reform efforts. The international community took the warning. Three days later, the UN evacuated most of its personnel from Haiti.

Guy Malary chose not to retreat, but rather to make a stand for justice in Haiti. He paid for his commitment with his life. So far, little, if anything, has been done to identify his killers or call them to account for the crime. Mr. Malary's colleagues at the Ministry of Justice have understandably been unwilling to run the same risks, having concluded that foreign governments will be unable or unwilling to protect them if the military and its allies should decide to strike again. Only with accountability — starting perhaps with the apprehension of Guy Malary's killers — will this calculus change and permit others to step forward as he did.

Each of the recipients of letters from the Lawyer-to-Lawyer Network on the Malary case — President Clinton, Secretary General Boutros-Ghali and Gen. Cédras — could and should have done more to protect and support Guy Malary and others like him in Haiti. Each of them is still in a position to make decisions which can promote or thwart the legacy of his efforts. On behalf of Guy Malary, the Haitian people, and all those in every nation whose security requires an institutionalized respect for law, we urge readers to write letters regarding the cases that are documented in this volume. National and international leaders must continue to hear calls for investigation and prosecution of human rights violations and a renewed priority for human rights in international policy. Guy Malary, and his colleagues in every Lawyer-to-Lawyer Network appeal, every edition of *In Defense of Rights*, deserve nothing less.

30 LAWYERS AND JUDGES KILLED IN 1993

ALGERIA

Mahfouz Bekai
President of Blida Military Court
Assassinated June 15

Ahmad Hambali
Professor of Islamic law, University of Tizi Ouzou
Shot dead by hooded gunmen, September 30

Mahfouz Kerdali
Algiers investigating magistrate
Assassinated November 30

Lakhdar Rouaz
President of Special Court, Oran
Assassinated December 6

Assistant Prosecutor
Algiers Special Court
Assassinated, details unknown

Chief Prosecutor
Tlemcen Special Court
Assassinated, details unknown

President
Kolea Special Court
Assassinated, details unknown

President
Tenes Special Court
Assassinated, details unknown

ARGENTINA

Lucio Dato
Vice President of Bar Association of Paraná
Tortured and murdered in his office, October

BRAZIL

Marcia María Eugenio de Carvalho
Lawyer in Pernambuco
Shot dead in her car by three hired gunmen, January 29

Paulo Coelho Pereira
Federal counsellor for the Brazilian Bar Association
Shot dead outside his home, February 19

COLOMBIA

Carlos Alberto Caicedo Méndez
Lawyer in La Palma, Cundinamarca
Assassinated by FARC guerrillas, October 8

Edgar Contreras Leal
Public Prosecutor's Office, Cucutá
Assassinated by militia, Barrancabermeja, April 27

Gerardo Daza García
Human rights lawyer in Tunja
Found hanged in his office, April 5

Eduardo Lancheros Abriú
Prosecutor General's Office of Antioquia
Assassinated by an unknown woman, Medellín, March 12

Freddy Yesid Martínez Murillo
Prosecutor General's Office of Antioquia
Tortured and killed by EPL guerrillas, February 4

Jesús Antonio Montoya Ospina
Human rights lawyer, Bogotá
Shot 14 times by unidentified gunmen, December 14

Jaime Benito Parrado
Prosecutor General's Office of Antioquia
Tortured and killed by EPL guerrillas, February 4

Ricardo Villa Salsedo
Lawyer and former senator
Shot dead by unknown assailants, January 8

EL SALVADOR

José Eduardo Pineda Valenzuela
Human Rights Ombudsman's Office
Died March 17
of injuries sustained in a 1992 attack

Francisco Arturo Pleitez Lemus
First Criminal Court Judge
Stabbed to death in front of his home, September 3

HAITI

Guy Malary
Minister of Justice
Shot dead outside his office in Port-au-Prince, October 14

INDIA

Kulwant Singh Saini
Attorney in Ropar, Punjab
Disappeared January 25, presumed dead

IRAQ

Jassem Mukhlis
Lawyer in Tikrit and former Iraqi ambassador
Executed, date unknown

NICARAGUA

Leonel González Vargas
Justice of the peace and human rights advocate
Murdered by unknown men, March 26

SENEGAL

Babacar Seye
Vice-President of Constitutional Council
Assassinated by "People's Army," May 15

SOUTH AFRICA

Phabo Molewa
Human rights attorney
Found dead in Johannesburg township, December 20

TURKEY

Metin Can
Lawyer, Elaziğ branch chairman of Human Rights Association (HRA)
Tortured and killed, late February

Şevket Epozdemir
Lawyer, HRA representative in Tatvan
Kidnapped, tortured, shot once in the head, November 25

ZAIRE

Pierre Ikomo Bamala
Military judge in Kinshasa
Killed at home by soldiers, June 2

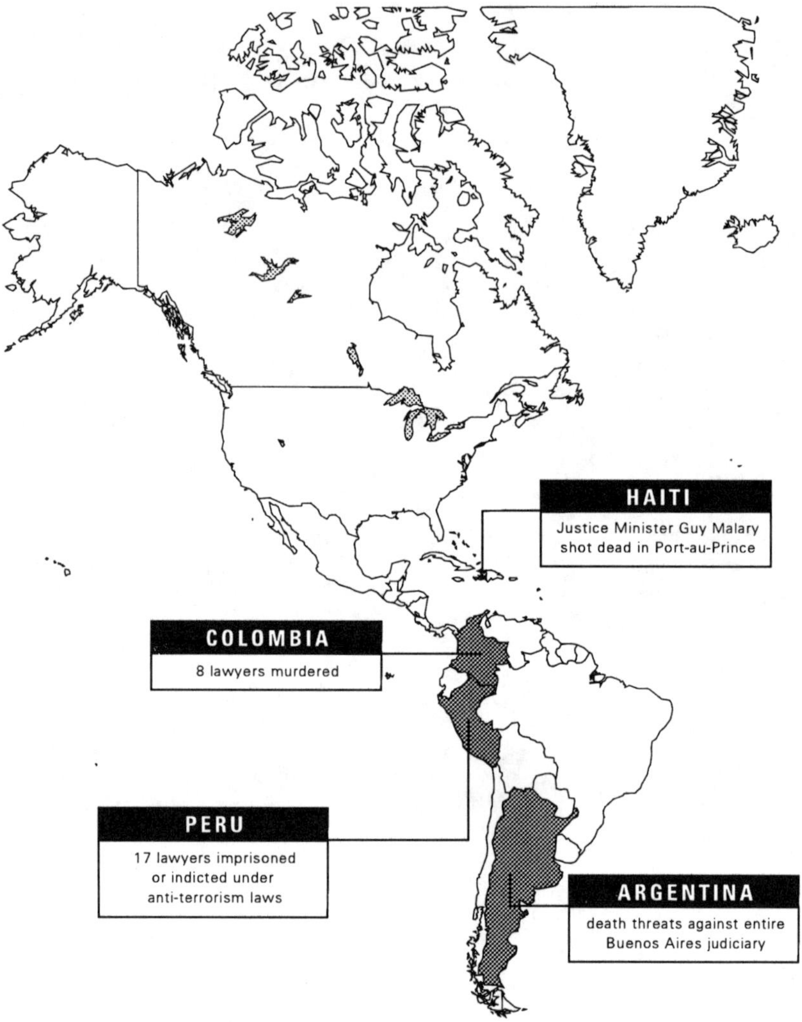
HAITI
Justice Minister Guy Malary shot dead in Port-au-Prince
COLOMBIA
8 lawyers murdered
PERU
17 lawyers imprisoned or indicted under anti-terrorism laws
ARGENTINA
death threats against entire Buenos Aires judiciary

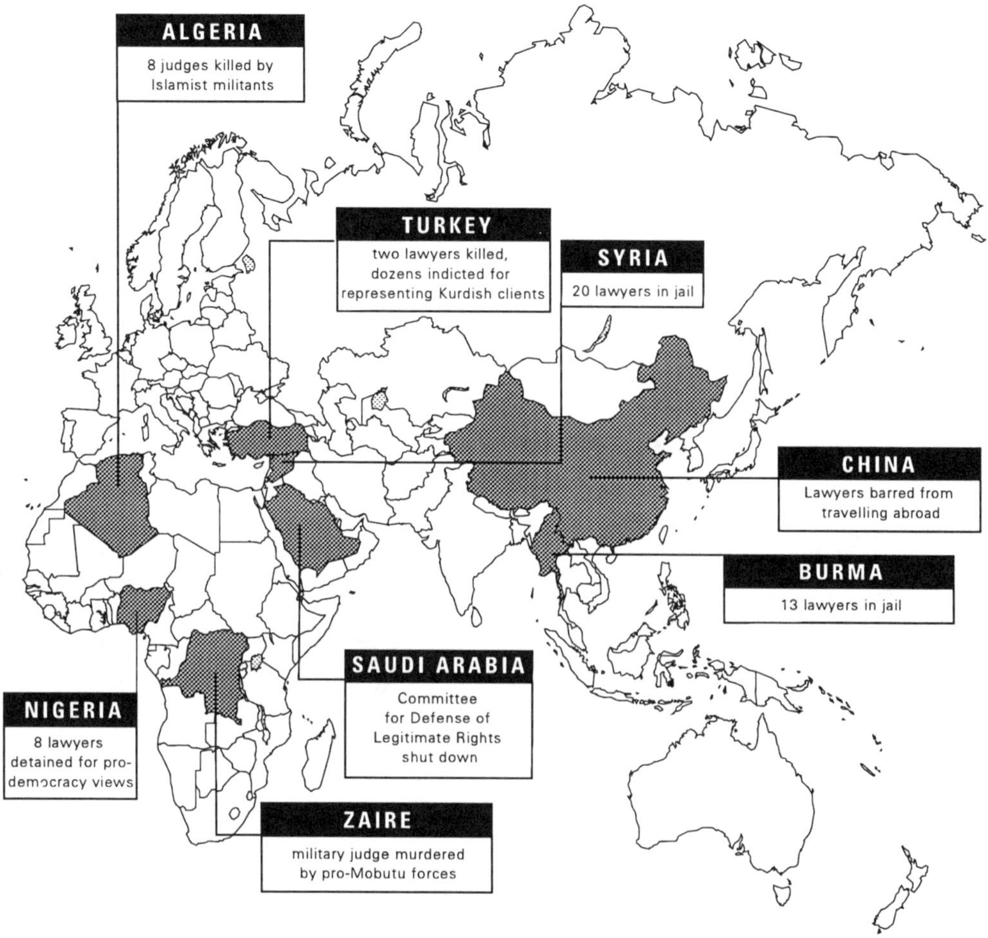
ALGERIA
8 judges killed by Islamist militants
TURKEY
two lawyers killed, dozens indicted for representing Kurdish clients
SYRIA
20 lawyers in jail
CHINA
Lawyers barred from travelling abroad
BURMA
13 lawyers in jail
SAUDI ARABIA
Committee for Defense of Legitimate Rights shut down
NIGERIA
8 lawyers detained for pro-democracy views
ZAIRE
military judge murdered by pro-Mobutu forces

GUATEMALA: CHALLENGE TO IMPUNITY —AND THE BACKLASH

BY ROBERT O. WEINER*

For human rights professionals, statistics alone are a suspect tool for gauging the scope and seriousness of a given situation. This is so for several reasons. First, numbers often reflect local investigative capacity more than they do the reality under investigation. Second, methodology and terminology are hardly uniform. The same can be said for the credibility of sources, and their willingness to come forward. Moreover, such factors can vary over time, perhaps giving the misleading appearance of underlying trends that may not in fact exist.

On occasion, however, the statistical variation from one year to the next may be so striking that it demands explanation. Guatemala in 1993 was just such a case. While the overall number of violations against lawyers and judges which came to the attention of the Lawyers Committee remained roughly constant within each region and worldwide, the number of incidents reported by reliable sources in Guatemala jumped from just 3 (involving 5 people) to no fewer than 16 (involving 37 individuals and two non-governmental legal groups).

Human rights observers point out that the overall level of human rights abuses reported in Guatemala during 1993 was roughly equivalent to the previous year. The sharp increase in cases involving legal professionals cannot then be understood simply as part of a

*Robert O. Weiner coordinates the Latin American and Caribbean program of the Lawyers Committee.

generally deteriorating human rights situation. Nor can it be explained by a dramatic increase in the number or capacity of groups documenting these incidents. It is the acts themselves, not their enhanced observation by others, that account for the dramatic statistical increase. Why then the increase in such acts of violence?

The answer appears to be a paradoxical one: the increasing level of attacks on the legal profession seems to be directly linked to the inroads that human rights advocacy has made in Guatemala in recent years. What has occurred might best be described as a response to pockets of progress in the administration of justice. Before 1993, only a handful of members of the security forces were ever tried and convicted for human rights crimes. The few convictions that did occur rarely survived appeal, even in the strongest cases. Members of the judiciary, aided and abetted by police and prosecutors, found innumerable ways to delay or avoid action in cases involving human rights abuses. And such judicial remedies as remained on the statute books were, in practice, virtually non-existent. One study found, for example, that judges failed to respond to more than 4,100 of the 5,729 habeas corpus petitions on file with the Guatemalan Supreme Court between July 1987 and December 1989.

During 1993, however, the number of pending and successful prosecutions in human rights cases increased. In a handful of precedent-setting cases, 1993 witnessed political violence on trial, with soldiers — and in some cases even officers — being convicted for plotting and carrying out death squad murders. Related events raised the possibility of even greater revelations and prosecutions. Several soldiers imprisoned for human rights crimes and embittered that they had been scapegoated for crimes ordered by their superiors, initially offered to testify in exchange for the possibility of leniency and physical protection. (Suspicious deaths of a number of prisoners soon followed, however, with a predictable decline in the amount of information being divulged.)

That some sectors of Guatemalan society would react violently against increased judicial activity over human rights matters is not surprising. Impunity has always rested on fear, and the present violent backlash seeks to rekindle the pervasive fear of reprisals that preempted assertions of judicial authority for so long. Among the cases listed in these pages are those of 18 Guatemalan judges, most of them in the unfamiliar position of passing civilian judgment on military personnel for human rights violations and narcotics trafficking. They were all victims of a classic Guatemalan tactic: the anonymous death squad warning.

Four of the judges received threats only days before affirming the convictions of military defendants in three well-known and highly controversial human rights cases: the *Los Traileros* massacre, in which eleven people were killed and dumped by the side of a highway; and the murders by military death squads of anthropologist Myrna Mack and US citizen Michael Devine. Magistrates Mario Guillermo Ruíz Wong, Héctor Hugo Pérez Aguilera and Mario René Diaz López received a stream of anonymous telephone threats and on April 23 an anonymous letter warning them that their days "are numbered" before the authors of the note would "apply their own law, that of the gun."

In October an anonymous death squad singled out Supreme Court President Juan José Rodil Peralta, accusing him of conspiring with Guatemalan and foreign guerrillas. At the time, Rodil was presiding over the Court's review of a petition to compel the continued investigation of the defendant's military superiors in connection with the Myrna Mack killing.

Because such threats resonate with a brutal recent past, they are to be taken seriously. Many Guatemalans still recall the eleven student activists who disappeared in July and August 1989 after they had been the target of anonymous death threats. In the case of those threatened during 1993, concern over possible international reaction to mass killings may have staved off actual violence so far. The judges involved are still in danger, however, and may represent targets of opportunity for those inclined to try to halt further prosecutions.

The threats against well-known judges in Guatemala City also serves the additional — and perhaps even the primary — purpose of serving notice on lesser figures who exist out of the national and international spotlight. The methodology of murder has clearly shifted in Guatemala. These days, the victims of actual physical attack, as opposed to the *threat* of attack, are less likely to be recognizable figures; the aim of deterrence is as readily served by reserving the real violence for those who will attract less international consternation. Hence a lawyer working for the Michael Devine family is threatened and then run off a highway and nearly killed; an attorney with the human rights Ombudsman's office in the northwestern town of Huehuetenango is kidnapped; a bomb explodes in the modest offices of a progressive lawyers' association.

By taking prompt action, whether through the Lawyer-to-Lawyer Network or other channels, lawyers in the United States can not only assist their individual colleagues, but also help to preserve the critical initiative that they and others have taken to reinvent in a meaningful way the functions of judges, prosecutors and lawyers. Their efforts have created an opening within Guatemala for increased accountability to the rule of law. Outside, our job is to foster and widen that opening.

POLITICAL VIOLENCE AND THE BREAKDOWN OF THE RULE OF LAW:

THE CASES OF ALGERIA AND EGYPT

BY NEIL HICKS*

Algeria's descent into armed confrontation between the military government and the Islamic Salvation Front (FIS) and its supporters, which has gathered pace since the cancellation of elections in January 1992, has devastated the Algerian justice system. Military courts, which had relinquished their jurisdiction over civilians in 1989, were reactivated after the events of January 1992, detracting from the competence of the civilian judiciary. After the first round of voting on December 26, 1991, the FIS was set to win a landslide victory that would have ended 30 years of single-party rule by the National Liberation Front. However, in order to pre-empt the formation of a FIS government, a military junta seized power, canceled the elections and installed a High State Council dominated by military officers. The FIS was banned, and thousands of its supporters imprisoned.

The new regime passed sweeping anti-terrorism legislation in September 1992, essentially prohibiting all criticism of the government. The new law provided for the creation of Special Courts, with civilian judges appointed by the President of the Republic. In April 1993, the anti-terrorism laws were further strengthened to give judges in the Special Courts powers to expel or suspend lawyers who "use dilatory and obstructionist maneuvers"

---

*Neil Hicks coordinates the Lawyers Committee's Middle East and North Africa program and its Freedom of Association project.

when appearing before them. Thus lawyers who presented a vigorous defense of their clients before a Special Court, where international fair trial standards were already violated by virtue of the direct appointment of judges by the executive branch, risked suspension from the legal profession for periods of up to one year.

Understandably, Algerian lawyers protested this interference in their ability to carry out their professional duties. Branches of the Algerian Bar Association in Annaba, Batna, Constantine and Algiers held meetings of their members at which they decided to boycott the Special Courts until these measures were suspended. The government responded by declaring these meetings illegal. It stated, implausibly: "These debates are not the prerogatives of general assemblies of lawyers, because they are not of a professional nature." On May 10, 1993, the Algerian government obtained a ruling from the administrative chamber of the Supreme Court placing an injunction on the implementation of any resolution to boycott the Special Courts by a bar association branch. The government's actions directly contradicted internationally agreed standards on the role of lawyers which provide:

> Lawyers, like other citizens, are entitled to freedom of expression, belief, association and assembly. In particular, they shall have the right to take part in public discussion of matters concerning the law, the administration of justice and the

> promotion and protection of human rights ...[3]

For the remainder of 1993, lawyers complied grudgingly with the Supreme Court ruling. For example, in the major trial of 58 defendants accused of placing a bomb at Boumédienne International Airport, before a Special Court, members of the defense team absented themselves from the hearings, or appeared late in court until threatened by suspension and even imprisonment by the President of the Court under the amended anti-terrorism law. During 1993, no actual suspensions of lawyers were reported, although in one case, 11 lawyers were ordered to be suspended by a judge in Algiers. Only after the intervention of the Algiers Branch of the bar association was the order lifted.

The Algerian judiciary paid a heavy price for the government's abuse of judicial authority for political purposes. At least seven judges and magistrates were among the more than 200 victims of killings attributed to armed opposition groups believed to be supporters of the FIS. FIS leaders abroad were equivocal in their statements about the campaign of violence directed against both civilians and members of the security forces in Algeria. At the same time, more than 500 suspected supporters of the Islamist opposition were killed by the security forces in 1993. The Lawyers Committee condemned all killings of civilians by armed opposition groups, as well as other killings which violated international human rights law.

While Algeria represented an extreme example of the rule of law disintegrating when caught between the competing pressures of violent opposition groups and a lawless government, similar trends

[3] UN Basic Principles on the Role of Lawyers, 1990, at Article 23.

were evident elsewhere in North Africa. In Egypt, at least 15 lawyers were held in administrative detention without charge or trial under State of Emergency legislation, apparently because of their activities in defense of prisoners accused of membership in Egypt's increasingly visible armed Islamist opposition groups. These cases were particularly disturbing because the detained lawyers had repeatedly obtained court orders for their release, only to see these orders overridden by the executive authority of the Ministry of the Interior.

The long-standing practice of courts in cases trying offenses under State of Emergency legislation having their verdicts countermanded by the executive branch undermines the independence and the authority of the Egyptian judiciary. This pernicious process was accelerated by President Hosni Mubarak's 1992 decision to grant military courts, presided over by military judges directly appointed by the Executive branch, jurisdiction over civilians accused of crimes involving political violence. This erosion of judicial independence, with the thinly veiled political purpose of clamping down on armed Islamist opposition groups, has led to a decline in the due process rights of Egyptian political detainees facing trial, and to a marked increase in the number of death sentences imposed by the Egyptian courts.

Armed Islamist opposition groups in Egypt have come to see the judiciary as indistinguishable from the coercive powers of the state. In a chilling echo of the conflagration that is now consuming Algeria, judges have thereby become targets for political violence. On November 1, 1993, the *Jihad* (Holy War) group stated that all those involved in the administration of the special military courts were to be considered "apostates", thus publicly declaring that military judges and prosecutors to be targets for political assassination.

The rule of law depends on a strong independent judiciary capable of holding state officials and security forces accountable to legal standards. When governments disregard judicial independence, using the courts to give a facade of legitimacy to the repression of their political opponents, the human rights of citizens are an early casualty. The cycle of violence fuelled by state lawlessness confronting increasingly desperate armed opposition groups makes the practice of law a hazardous pursuit. In Egypt, as in other countries such as Turkey and Peru, lawyers who seek to represent suspected supporters of armed opposition groups themselves become victims of the wide-ranging repressive measures designed to combat terrorism. Thus lawyers are charged with violent offenses or subject to administrative detention without charge or trial because they are identified with the clients they represent. This in turn may discourage the great majority of lawyers from representing unpopular clients accused of political violence, further removing legal protections and safeguards from suspected political opponents.

Civil peace, public order and fundamental human rights cannot survive the assault on the justice system that has occurred in Algeria, nor the erosion of legal safeguards we are witnessing today in Egypt. The process must be arrested and the rule of law reasserted if the physical and professional integrity of legal professionals is to be maintained.

AFRICA

RENE DEGNY SEGUI TRAVEL DENIED

René Dégny Ségui is dean of the law faculty at the University of Abidjan and president of the Ivory Coast Human Rights League (*Ligue Ivoirienne des Droits de l'Homme*). As reported in last year's edition of *In Defense of Rights*, he was arrested after a February 1992 demonstration that called for the prosecution of military officials responsible for human rights violations. He was sentenced to two years imprisonment in March 1992, but released five months later under an amnesty.

Professor Ségui's difficulties continued in 1993, however. Ivory Coast nationals require government authorization before travelling abroad, but Professor Ségui was denied permission to travel on four separate occasions. One of these prohibitions forced him to cancel his planned attendance at the June 1993 World Conference on Human Rights in Vienna. He was also forbidden to travel to Strasbourg to teach courses at the Institute for Human Rights.

KENYA

AHMED NASIR ABDULLAHI ASSAULTED, DETAINED

According to the Centre for the Independence of Judges and Lawyers of the International Commission of Jurists, lawyer and law professor Ahmednasir M. Abdullahi was assaulted and detained briefly on May 26, 1993. Mr. Abdullahi reportedly arrived at

Nairobi's Central Police Station on that date to visit a client in detention. When he asked to see the list of detainees, the officer in charge refused. When Mr. Abdullahi insisted, the officer struck him in the head. He was then detained overnight on charges of creating a disturbance.

MIRUGI KARIUKI INDICTED

Mirugi Kariuki is a human rights lawyer living and working in the Nakuru area of Kenya. His clients include many victims of ethnic violence in that region; he has also represented a number of individuals who claim to have been victims of human rights abuses by the Kenya African National Union (KANU) government. His recent clients include thirteen opposition members of parliament charged with entering an area proscribed for reasons of security.

On September 18, 1993, Mr. Kariuki, his wife and brother were stopped by police as they drove to visit a relative in the town of Eldoret, north of Nairobi. Mr. Kariuki personally witnessed the search of his vehicle at the police station where he was detained; nothing was found. Nevertheless, Mr. Kariuki was later told that he was to be charged with possession of firearms that were supposedly discovered in the trunk of his car. He also faced the additional charges of entering a proscribed area and possessing seditious publications. On October 19, 1993, Mr. Kariuki was released on bail but forbidden to enter the "restricted security zone" of Nakuru district. He was also obliged to report twice a week to the Nakuru police. His case is being handled by the distinguished Kenyan lawyer and human rights advocate Gibson Kamau Kuria.

This is not the first time that Mr. Kariuki has faced similar charges. As reported in the 1992 edition of *In Defense of Rights*, Mr. Kariuki and fellow-lawyer Rumba Kinuthia (see below) were arrested in October 1990 and charged with possession of firearms for the purpose of overthrowing the government. The two men were detained for more than two years until January 1993, when the government dropped the treason charges and released them. Mr. Kariuki also spent two-and-a-half years in jail without charge between December 1986 and mid-1989.

RUMBA KINUTHIA HARASSED

Since his release from prison in January 1993 (see above), Rumba Kinuthia has suffered serious health problems. According to Amnesty International, Mr. Kinuthia spent the last nine months of his detention in Kenyatta Hospital. At first he was chained to his bed by the wrist for 24 hours a day; after a visit by Amnesty International, this was reduced to twelve hours a day. He was under heavy guard, severely mistreated and frequently beaten.

On his release in January 1993, he was admitted to the private Nairobi Hospital and later to the Mater Misericordia hospital, where he was treated for the effects of his detention and mistreatment. He now faces some 400,000 Kenya Shillings (about $6,150) in unpaid medical bills. Mr. Kinuthia has lost more than half his former clients as a result of being stigmatized by the government as an "advocate." He has also been repeatedly denied permission from the authorities to hold a fundraising event, or *harambee*, to revive his law practice.

PAUL MUITE ASSAULTED, HARASSED

Paul Muite, chairman of the Law Society of Kenya and first vice-chairman of the opposition Forum for the Restoration of Democracy (FORD), was beaten by police on April 6, 1993, while taking part in a demonstration to protest the economic situation in Kenya. Mr. Muite had also been beaten on at least two previous occasions in 1991 and 1992 (see *In Defense of Rights 1992*).

Mr. Muite continues to complain of systematic harassment by the authorities, asserting that his movements are monitored and his telephone tapped. His car has been attacked on at least three occasions in 1993: once when Special Branch officers vandalized it in broad daylight; once when a rock was thrown through the window, narrowly missing Mr. Muite's three children; and once when a bucket of human feces was thrown at it. The Centre for the Independence of Judges and Lawyers also reports that agents of Kenya's Criminal Investigations Department attempted to arrest Mr. Muite on February 1, 1993, in response to a press statement that he had issued decrying a breakdown of security in the Northeastern Province.

JAMES ORENGO ASSAULTED

According to the Centre for the Independence of Judges and Lawyers, lawyer James Orengo, a member of parliament and secretary of constitutional and legal affairs for FORD, was attacked by police dogs on March 23, 1993 at a seminar on the resettlement of victims of politically instigated ethnic clashes. On April 6, 1993, he was beaten and injured by police after leading prayers at a demonstration.

TAIB ALI TAIB ASSAULTED, INDICTED

Taib Ali Taib is a human rights lawyer living and working in the port city of Mombasa. In the early morning hours of December 5, 1993, he was called to the home of a client and arrived to find it surrounded by police demanding to search the house. When the police declined to produce a search warrant, Mr. Taib refused them entry. The standoff continued until noon, when the police finally departed the scene. As they left, an officer warned Mr. Taib that "he would be dealt with."

When Mr. Taib arrived at his office at 7:15 a.m. the following day, December 6, he found a policeman waiting for him. When he demanded to know the officer's business, a number of other police entered the room, closed the door and proceeded to threaten and shove Mr. Taib and beat him with sticks. They then produced a number of pamphlets which they said were seditious, claiming to have found these in the office. Mr. Taib was taken to the police station and charged with sedition. His case has been filed in the High Court in Mombasa, where he is represented by human rights advocate Gibson Kamau Kuria.

NG'ANG'A THIONG'O HARASSED, CLIENT ACCESS DENIED

In July 1992, advocate Ng'ang'a Thiong'o undertook the pro bono representation of Francis Kipyego Rotich, who was charged with sedition for making a derogatory remark about police officers. Mr. Rotich was detained until September 1993, when he was found not guilty of the charge and released. Mr. Thiong'o was repeatedly harassed in trying to gain access to his client at the detention center at

Nyeri in order to prepare his case. On several occasions, he was only allowed to meet with his client in the final few minutes of visiting time. In direct contravention of the Prison Act (CAP 90 of the Laws of Kenya), Section V, 59 (3), prison officers would refuse to grant Mr. Thiong'o privacy to speak with his client. (The Act states that the advocate has a right to communicate with his/her client "in the sight but not in the hearing of a prison officer.") In this way, Mr. Thiong'o's ability to prepare a defense was effectively restricted to whispered exchanges in the courtroom immediately prior to the hearings.

MALAWI

FRIDAY MAKUTA RESIGNED

Malawian Minister of Justice Friday Makuta resigned on March 23, 1993, citing threats to the independence of the judiciary. In particular, Mr. Makuta complained that he had been asked to influence court decisions regarding the state and the ruling Malawi Congress Party.

MAURITANIA

LAWYERS COLLECTIVE OF WIDOWS AND VICTIMS OF ASSASSINATION, TORTURE AND DISAPPEARANCE FROM THE EVENTS OF 1990-1991 HARASSED

The Lawyers Collective (*Collectif des Avocats des Veuves et Rescapés des Assassinats, Tortures et Disparitions des Evénements de 1990-1991*) is a group of some 22 lawyers representing families of victims of ethnic purges by the Mauritanian military. In 1990 and 1991, the government conducted a systematic campaign to remove members of the Black-African community from positions of influence in Mauritania's government and armed forces, and to expel them from fertile land in the Senegal River valley in southern Mauritania. The campaign targeted members of the Hal Pulaar, Sonicke and other ethnic groups not affiliated with Mauritania's Arab population, which has controlled the country since its independence from France in 1960. More than 500 black Mauritanians were executed without trial or due process during the campaign.

Members of the Lawyers Collective have tried to seek redress for those affected by the purges and mass killings. The government, meanwhile, has taken various steps to impede the judicial process and block the Collective's efforts. It has also taken reprisals against a number of individual members of the Collective.

Harassment of the Lawyers Collective during 1993 has taken many forms, including the following:

The National Assembly overwhelmingly approved a resolution denouncing the legal action taken by the Collective, challenging the patriotism of the lawyers involved, and encouraging the Prime Minister to take appropriate action in response.

Beginning in March 1993, the government began a coordinated effort to terminate contracts between the government or state-owned enterprises and lawyers belonging to the Collective. Although most of its members come from the ranks of the Black African legal community, this effort particularly affected Arab members. Mauritania is an extremely poor country, and the government is involved in virtually every area of economic and social activity. Consequently, this campaign threatened the livelihood of the lawyers who were singled out. Among the lawyers who lost specific contracts were the following:

DIALLO YACOUB	SONELEC (state water and electricity utility); SONIMEX (import and export company); Finance Ministry; Société Algéro-Mauritanienne des Pêches (ALMAP). The total value of these contracts was almost $200,000.
BRAHIM OULD EBETTY	SNCP (fish processing company); SAMIN (leather and gold works).
AHMED OULD CHEICHKSIDYA	OPT (post and telecommunications);
YARBA OULD CHEICHKSIDYA	SNCPP (petroleum products).

The *Cabinet Yarba et Ahmed Ould Cheichksidya* was also one of at least two law offices forced to close temporarily when the government selectively enforced provisions of the Mauritanian tax code to the detriment of lawyers who belonged to the Collective. The other firm affected was the *Cabinet Ichidou*.

On May 29, 1993, in the name of national unity and "harmony," the Mauritanian government issued an amnesty covering all offenses committed by the security forces between 1989 and 1992.

BELLO AIDELOJE DETAINED

Bello Aideloje, a Lagos-based lawyer, was arrested at the end of September 1993 for distributing leaflets calling for strikes and demonstrations to protest the military government's cancellation of the June 12 elections, widely believed to have been won by Moshood K.O. Abiola. He was subsequently released without charge. Mr. Aideloje was affiliated with the Campaign for Democracy (CD), a national coalition of human rights groups, trade unions, student organizations and other civic groups that came together in May 1992 to press then Head of State Gen. Ibrahim Babangida to return the country to civilian rule.

FEMI FALANA DETAINED

Femi Falana, president of the National Association of Democratic Lawyers (NADL), a member organization of the Campaign for Democracy, was arrested at least three times during 1993, on March 9, April 16 and July 6. On the first two occasions he was quickly released without being charged, and with no explanation. Mr. Falana was arrested for the third time on July 6 in connection with his involvement with the Campaign for Democracy, in particular its demand for the results of the June 12 to be made public. He was charged on July 12 with sedition and conspiracy to incite violence under the State Security (Detention of Persons) Decree of 1984 ("Decree 2"), before being released on August 29. Mr. Falana is also an active member of the Committee for the Defense of Human Rights (CDHR). Earlier arrests and proceedings against Mr. Falana are detailed in the 1992 edition of *In Defense of Rights*.

CHIEF GANI FAWEHINMI DETAINED

Chief Gani Fawehinmi, a leading member of both the Nigerian legal community and the Nigerian human rights movement, was arrested on July 3, released the same day, and then rearrested on July 6 under Decree 2, together with Femi Falana. (See also *In Defense of Rights 1992*.) Also arrested a day earlier, on July 5, were CD chairman and CDHR president Dr. Beko Ransome-Kuti, and two other CD members, Baba Omojola and Segun Maiyegun. All five men were transferred to Wuse police station in Abuja, where they were held incommunicado under Decree 2, which allows for indefinite detention, renewable at six-week intervals. On July 12 they were charged with sedition and conspiracy to incite violence (see above). On August 29 this entire group of detainees was released on compassionate grounds by Ernest Shonekan, who headed the short-lived Interim National Government from August to November 1993.

On August 9, while Chief Fawehinmi was in detention, State Security Service agents raided his office, ordered staff to leave, searched the premises, and seized materials used in the preparation of the Nigerian Weekly Law Reports as well as published records of Supreme Court judgments.

TITUS MANN ARRESTED

Lawyer Titus Mann is the coordinator of the Civil Liberties

Organization (CLO) in Plateau State and Middle Belt regional coordinator for the Campaign for Democracy. He was arrested on August 10, 1993 for distributing pamphlets and other literature calling for peaceful demonstrations to protest the cancellation of the June 12 presidential election. No further details are known of his detention.

JOHN MATTHEW ARRESTED

Attorney John Matthew is a member of the Civil Liberties Organization, based in its northern office in Kaduna, and a co-founder with Festus Okoye (see below) of Human Rights Monitors, a group that is also based in northern Nigeria. Mr. Matthew was arrested at the end of June 1993 for distributing CD literature calling for non-violent protests over the cancellation of the June 12 election. No further details are known of his detention.

LEDUM MITEE DETAINED

Lawyer Ledum Mitee, deputy president of the Movement for the Survival of the Ogoni People (MSOP), was detained six times in 1993. On the last of these occasions, he was taken from his home in the early hours of the morning of December 28 and held at an undisclosed location until January 4, 1994. The MSOP has clashed with government authorities, as well as with the oil companies Shell Oil and Shell Nigeria, over environmental pollution in the oil-producing lands of Rivers State, where the Ogoni people live.

FESTUS OKOYE ARRESTED, TRAVEL DENIED

Festus Okoye is the former chairman of the Civil Liberties Organization, based in its Kaduna office. He is also, with John

Matthew (see above), co-founder of Human Rights Monitors. In addition, Mr. Okoye was secretary of the Nigerian Bar Association from 1991 until June 1993.

Mr. Okoye was arrested without a warrant at his office in Turaki Ali House in Kaduna on August 10, 1993. He was taken to the State Security Service complex at police headquarters and forced to strip. After being interrogated, he was placed in solitary confinement in a maggot-infested cell measuring four feet by six, with no ventilation or toilet facilities. The next day, Mr. Okoye was taken to his home and office, where security agents searched his colleagues and took away personal correspondence, which was not returned. Mr. Okoye was then returned to solitary confinement. Three days later, on August 14, SSS agents accused him of treason and conspiring with the U.S. consulate in Kaduna, but no formal charges were brought against him. After the Nigerian Bar Association had filed a habeas corpus petition on Mr. Okoye's behalf, the Kaduna High Court eventually ordered his release on August 14. On August 27, Mr. Okoye was again detained, this time at Lagos's Murtala Muhammed Airport as he was preparing to travel to the United States to pursue his legal studies. Officials from the Immigration Services and SSS agents also seized his passport. This was later returned, but only after Mr. Okoye was told that he was on a list of persons forbidden to leave the country.

CHIEF MIKE OZEHKHOME DETAINED

Chief Mike Ozehkhome, a lawyer and president of a Nigerian non-governmental organization called the Universal Defenders of Democracy, was briefly detained on July 2, 1993 together with Dr.

Beko Ransome-Kuti, president of the Committee for the Defense of Human Rights and chairman of the Campaign for Democracy. Like Dr. Ransome-Kuti, Chief Ozehkhome was detained for asking the Babangida government to release the results of the June 12 elections. He was released without charges.

CHIMA UBANI HARASSED

Lawyer Chima Ubani, campaign director for the Civil Liberties Organization and secretary of the Campaign for Democracy, was a target of official harassment throughout 1993. On February 26, security forces raided his home as part of a sweep that included the CLO's national headquarters in the Surulere section of Lagos, as well as the home of CLO president Olisa Agbakoba. On March 10, SSS agents again raided the CLO office, demanding to know Mr. Ubani's whereabouts. On July 10, SSS agents raided the home of Dr. Beko Ransome-Kuti, once more looking for Mr. Ubani.

DR. ONJE GYE WADO ARRESTED

Dr. Onje Gye Wado, a lecturer at the law faculty at the University of Jos in Plateau State, was arrested in July after organizing Campaign for Democracy protests over the cancelled June 12 elections. Dr. Gye Wado is also the secretary of the Plateau State branch of the Civil Liberties Organization.

NIGERIAN BAR ASSOCIATION GOVERNMENT INTERFERENCE

The Nigerian Bar Association has long been a vocal critic of the military-controlled transition to civilian rule. It has voiced its opposition to the continual delays in the transition process and frequently protested abuses of the rule of law by the Babangida government. With the detention on May 2, 1992, of Chief Gani Fawehinmi, Femi Falana and Dr. Beko Ransome-Kuti, who were held incommunicado under Decree 2, the relationship hit a new low. A Lagos High Court ordered the defendants to be produced in court, but the ruling was ignored by the government. In protest, the Lagos branch of the NBA boycotted the courts until the government reversed its decision. In March 1993, the government took the opportunity to intervene when the NBA was divided by a dispute over who should be its acting president. At that time, Gen. Babangida introduced Decree 21, which dissolved the existing leadership of the bar and appointed a caretaker committee to run it. Only after the appointment of Olu Onugurwa as Attorney General in November 1993 was the decree finally repealed.

RWANDA

ALPHONSE-MARIE NKUBITO — ATTACKED

On November 14, 1993, unidentified assailants threw hand grenades at Alphonse-Marie Nkubito, Attorney General of the Kigali Court of Appeal and president of the non-governmental Rwandan Human Rights Association (*Association Rwandaise pour les Droits de l'Homme*, or ARDHO). Mr. Nkubito was seriously injured in the attack, which took place as he was entering his home in the Kacyiru suburb of the Rwandan capital, Kigali. According to Amnesty International, the attackers are thought to have been members of the security forces acting clandestinely. Mr. Nkubito was about to act as prosecutor in the trial of a local businessman accused of the theft of relief supplies to victims of the ethnic civil war that has raged since October 1990 between the majority Hutu and the minority Tutsi. The businessman was known to have close ties to the Rwandan security forces and to senior officials in the Hutu-dominated government of President Juvénal Habyarimana.

While Mr. Nkubito was recovering from his wounds in hospital, neighbors witnessed armed men attempting to break into his home on several occasions. Fearing that he would be killed, Mr. Nkubito fled the hospital and went into hiding. Numerous other human rights advocates in Rwanda also received death threats or were the victims of physical attack during 1993.

JUDGE MATHIEU UWIZEYE ATTACKED

In November 1993, Judge Mathieu Uwizeye, president of the court of Kibungo, escaped a simulated road accident staged by militia loyal to the ruling Republican Movement for Democracy and Development (*Mouvement Républicain National pour la Démocratie et le Développement*, or MRND). The government had earlier criticized Judge Uwizeye for cooperating with foreign observers investigating violations of human rights in Rwanda between 1990 and 1993. In particular, Judge Uwizeye had denounced the massacre of more than 300 civilians by government forces at Nasho.

SENEGAL

BABACAR SEYE KILLED

Babacar Seye, vice president of Senegal's Constitutional Council, was assassinated on May 15, 1993. According to the Centre for the Independence of Judges and Lawyers, the killing was apparently in retaliation for the Council's controversial refusal to rule on the disputed results of February 1993 presidential elections. Responsibility for the killing was claimed by a group calling itself the People's Army. In a telephone message to a Senegalese newspaper, the group said that the murder of Babacar Seye was a "warning to other magistrates of the Constitutional Council so that they will actually respect the people's will."

The Constitutional Council is part of a new Senegalese court system adopted in 1992, together with the Court of Cassation and the Council of State. It was invited to rule on the 1993 presidential elections after the National Electoral Commission disagreed on the results. The head of the Constitutional Council, Keba Mbaye, declined to do so, saying that this kind of intervention did not fall within the Council's jurisdiction. Mbaye resigned as President of the Constitutional Council on March 3, 1993.

PHABO MOLEWA KILLED

Phabo Molewa, a prominent human rights attorney, was found dead in Thakoza township outside Johannesburg on December 20, 1993, ten days after his family had reported him missing. According to police reports, Mr. Molewa had been killed by a single gunshot fired at close range. His body had been dumped in Thakoza after being killed elsewhere.

Mr. Molewa was a well-known lawyer in Johannesburg, and was also known as a mediator between rival political factions in the townships of the East Rand. On behalf of the Independent Mediation Service of South Africa (IMSA), he mediated disputes between labor unions and employers, between rival civic groups, and between political parties, including the African National Congress (ANC) and the Inkatha Freedom Party of Chief Mangosethu Buthelezi. On the day of his disappearance, Mr. Molewa was scheduled to mediate a civic association election dispute. Although the South African police have treated Mr. Molewa's murder as a common crime, his family believes that it was politically motivated, and the ANC has hired private investigators to look into his death.

SAMUEL NKOSI HARASSED

Samuel Nkosi is a partner in the firm of Nkosi and Associates in the town of Vrijheid is the northern part of Natal Province. He is an attorney of the Supreme Court of South Africa, Natal Provincial Division. His practice focusses primarily on human rights advocacy in an area dominated by conservative Afrikaners and the Inkatha Freedom Party. Mr. Nkosi, who is also a member of the ANC, is the only attorney in this part of South Africa who performs such human rights advocacy on a pro bono basis. Most of his clients are supported by the South African Legal Defense Fund. He has represented trade unions in arbitration, worked on cases involving the forced eviction and displacement of black tenant farmers, and represented individuals in complaints against the South African and Kwa Zulu police forces.

On September 17, 1993, the Natal Law Society filed an application before the Natal Supreme Court to have Mr. Nkosi disbarred. The Law Society's affidavit cites seven counts of "unprofessional, dishonorable or unworthy conduct," including irregularities in Mr. Nkosi's bookkeeping. According to Mr. Nkosi's attorney, the action against him is politically motivated and is designed to intimidate him and destroy his law practice and his human rights advocacy. In view of his inability to secure pro bono counsel, the Lawyers for Lawyers Foundation (*Stichting Advocaten voor Advocaten*), a non-governmental organization based in Amsterdam, has agreed to aid Mr. Nkosi with the cost of his defense.

SUDAN

ABDUL MAHMOUD HAJ-SALIH
ABDUL WAHAB AL-SHARA'NI — DETAINED

Abdul Mahmoud Haj-Salih, 47, a former Attorney General of Sudan, was arrested in March 1993 along with Umma Party activist

Abdul Wahab al-Shara'ni, aged 45. Both men are lawyers in the capital, Khartoum. Their arrests appear to have been part of a concerted effort by the Sudanese government to suppress independent advocacy in the lead-up to the March 15 elections for the Council of the Bar Association. (see below) Mr. Haj-Salih and Mr. al-Shara'ni were taken to a one of the secret detention centers in Khartoum known as "ghost houses," where detainees are habitually beaten upon arrival and tortured during interrogation. They were released without charge several days later. According to the Arab Lawyers Union, such brief periods of detention and torture without charge, ranging from about two weeks to as much as six months, are an increasingly common tactic used by the ruling National Salvation Revolutionary Command Council to harass perceived critics and political opponents.

HAMID MUHAMMAD HAMID DETAINED

According to Amnesty International, Hamid Muhammad Hamid, a 47-year-old lawyer and member of the Political Bureau and Central Committee of the Umma Party, was arrested on April 12, 1993. He was released without charge in May 1993. No further details of the case are available.

SAYED AHMED AL-HUSSEIN DETAINED, TRAVEL DENIED

Sayed Ahmed al-Hussein is a prominent Sudanese lawyer and Secretary General of the banned Democratic Unionist Party, as well as being a former Deputy Prime Minister and Minister of the Interior. He had been tried and acquitted in 1992 for allegedly plotting with the Sudan People's Liberation Army to overthrow the government (see *In Defense of Rights 1992*). He was detained on two further occasions in 1993. In July he was arrested and taken to a "ghost house." During his detention, he was forbidden to receive any visitors, including members of his family. He was eventually released without charge. Mr. al-Hussein was arrested again on November 19 after taking part in a student-organized symposium on the theme of "Peace in Sudan." He was once more released without charge in December, but remains under surveillance by the authorities and is prevented from travelling abroad.

SIDIK KADODA INDICTED, FLED COUNTRY

Sidik Kadoda, a 43-year-old lawyer in Khartoum, was arrested in November 1993 and charged with attempted adultery and possession and consumption of alcohol, both of which are criminal offenses under Islamic law (*Shari'a*) as observed in Sudan. The Arab Lawyers Union and the Sudan Human Rights Organization believe, however, that these were trumped-up charges designed to punish Mr. Kadoda for his work as a volunteer attorney defending college students charged with planning terrorist acts. The students had reportedly been subjected to severe torture for more than two years of their detention in a "ghost house." After Mr. Kadoda had petitioned the court to intervene to stop the torture of the students, his home was invaded by security police at 3 a.m. Finding him in the company of a woman who was not a legal relative, they took him to a police station and detained him overnight. The following day, a court released Mr. Kadoda on bail of one million Sudanese pounds (approximately US$10,000) while the prosecution was adjourned to prepare its case. Mr. Kadoda fled the country that same day and is now living in Egypt.

TAG ELSIR MUHAMMAD SALIH ARRESTED

According to the Arab Lawyers Union, lawyer Tag Elsir Muhammad Salih, former Minister of Foreign Affairs and a member of the Political Bureau of the banned Democratic Unionist Party, was arrested several times during 1993 and accused of conspiring to overthrow the government. No further details of this case are available.

OSMAN OMAR AL SHARIF DETAINED

Former Sudanese Minister of Justice and Attorney General Osman Omar Al Sharif, aged 48, was arrested on November 27, 1993 and accused of instigating a one-day strike by shopkeepers in the Central State city of Wad Medani. According to the Arab Lawyers Union, Mr. Al Sharif's arrest was part of a broader attempt to stifle political dissent. A member of the Political Bureau of the banned Democratic Unionist Party, Mr. Al Sharif was taken to a "ghost house," where he was kept until his release in mid-December. This was the third time that Mr. Al Sharif has been arrested since the present government took power in 1989.

SUDANESE BAR ASSOCIATION GOVERNMENT INTERFERENCE

After the military coup of January 1989, in a concerted attack on the independence of the legal profession, the Sudanese Bar Association was dissolved, together with the non-governmental Sudanese Human Rights Organization and the Sudan Legal Aid Association. From 1989-1993 the Bar Council was run by a steering committee made up exclusively of government-appointed supporters of the National Islamic Front (NIF). In March 1992, however, the government announced that it would modify the Advocates Act of 1993 to allow for fresh elections to the Bar Council. The March 15 vote was heavily boycotted by Sudanese lawyers, and all seats on the council were won by NIF militants. The new committee was not recognized by the Arab Lawyers Union (ALU), the umbrella organization of all bar associations in Arab countries, which concluded that the elections had failed to meet international legal standards. After the Bar Council election, the Sudanese government barred a number of lawyers not affiliated with the NIF from attending the Eighteenth General Council of the ALU in Morocco on May 20-23, 1993.

SUDANESE LAWYERS AND JUDGES — ARRESTED, DISMISSED

The Lawyers Committee has also received information from the Arab Lawyers Union of a number of other Sudanese lawyers and judges detained, arrested or dismissed from their posts during 1993. We believe that the following cases are representative of a much larger number of legal professionals harassed as a result of their professional activities. While additional information on these cases is not available, we include them as an indication of the gravity and extent of the harassment of the legal profession in Sudan.

KAMAL ALDIN HUSSEIN MUHAMMAD AHMED — Lawyer detained for six months on accusation of membership of the Ba'ath Party; subsequently released.

NASR ALDIN YOUSIF DAF ALLA — Assistant judge, dismissed after criticizing government policies on the confiscation of private property.

IHSAN FAKHRY — Appellate Court judge, dismissed.

NADIA MUSA AL-GANDAJLLY — First Instance magistrate, dismissed.

ALLA ALDIN AHMED HUSSEIN — Lawyer arrested and later released.

ABDEL RAHIEM MOHAMMED IRAKI — First class magistrate dismissed and detained for three weeks; also refused notarization powers by the authorities.

SWAZILAND

DOMINIC MNGOMEZULU
BENEDICT TSABEDZE — IMPRISONED

Lawyers Dominic Mngomezulu and Benedict Tsabedze both attended a rally in Nkaba on March 21, 1993, organized by the People's United Democratic Movement of Swaziland (PUDEMO) and the Swaziland Youth Congress (SWAYCO). To prevent the rally from taking place, police arrested 60 of the participants and assaulted several others. Mr. Mngomezulu and Mr. Tsabedze appeared at the Lobamba Circuit Magistrates Court on April 27 to represent the 60 defendants. However, on arriving in court the two lawyers were informed that they too were under arrest, along with those they had come to defend, on charges of holding an illegal political demonstration. They were, however, permitted to continue representing their clients as well as to conduct their own defense. All 62 defendants were granted bail, but were forbidden from engaging in any political activity or from speaking in any public forum. In addition, several defendants had their passports confiscated.

After the initial hearing on April 27, the case against Mr. Mngomezulu, Mr. Tsabedze and their fellow defendants was postponed until July 28, when evidence against them was presented. On August 20, all the defendants were found guilty and given suspended sentences of three months. Their appeals are pending.

MAGISTRATES ASSOCIATION OF SWAZILAND
MCABANGO DLAMINI
SIPHO MABUZA
DUMSANI MAGAGULA
STANLEY MAPHALALA
LUCAS MAZIYA
SABELO MNGOMEZULU
KENNETH NKAMBULE
DORIS TSHABALALA
KUSH VILAKATI
REUBEN ZONDI HARASSED, DISCIPLINARY ACTION

In July or August 1993, the Ministry of Justice of Swaziland appointed a special committee of the Judicial Service Commission, with the ostensible task of evaluating the performance of Swazi magistrates. The committee was made up of the country's Acting Director of Public Prosecutions, Minister of Justice, Attorney General, Commissioner of Police and other officials. On his appointment as King's Representative on the special committee, Mr. Thulani Masina of the Swaziland Law Society complained that the body had a "secret agenda" of targeting certain magistrates for removal from office. Mr. Masina pointed to the lack of a legal basis for the committee's actions and criticized it for proposing to remove magistrates without a fair hearing.

On August 2, following Mr. Masina's remarks, all thirteen members of the Magistrates Association of Swaziland went on strike to demand the dissolution of the special committee, with the exception of two magistrates from South Africa. At the same time, the Law Society of Swaziland condemned the new body as "totally undesirable, unconstitutional and contrary to the rule of law." In response, the Judicial Service Commission threatened to fire all of the striking magistrates, and on August 13 the Chief Justice of Swaziland charged the ten named above with disciplinary offenses under Regulation 26 (1) of the Judicial Service Commission Regulations of 1968. After three weeks, the magistrates were forced to return to work, and some were reportedly later fined.

ZAIRE

JUSTICE BALANDA MIKWIN LELIEL ATTACKED

Justice Balanda Mikwin Leliel is the 54-year-old President of the

Supreme Court of Zaire. On July 24, 1993, while the judge was at home with his family in the Kinsuka district of the capital, Kinshasa, his house was attacked by military police of the Division Spéciale Présidentielle (DSP), a force loyal to President Sese Seko Mobutu. The attack began at 9:00 p.m. and lasted seven hours, but police were unable to enter the house because of the presence of six bodyguards who had been hired by Justice Balanda. Although the judge telephoned for official help several times, no one came to his assistance or took any action to stop the attack. Justice Balanda's family subsequently went into hiding for several days.

Human rights advocates in Zaire believe that the attack on Justice Balanda was connected to a controversial case involving the constitutional right of Jehovah's Witnesses to practice their religion freely. In its constitutional interpretation of the case, the Supreme Court referred to the new Zairian Transitional Constitutional Act adopted by a National Conference under Prime Minister Etienne Tshisekedi wa Mulumba, rather than the Second Constitution of Zaire adopted under Mobutu. Before the armed attack on his house, pro-Mobutu forces had criticized Justice Balanda for failing to compel judges under his supervision to demonstrate loyalty to the president.

ROGER CIMANGA HARASSED

Roger Cimanga is a public prosecutor in the Jili District of Kinshasa, the Zairian capital, and a member of the Black Robes (*Toges Noires*), a human rights organization made up of Zairian magistrates and lawyers. In 1993, Mr. Cimanga assisted representatives of the U.S.-based human rights organization Africa Watch during a mission to Zaire to inspect conditions in prisons and police lockups. Shortly afterwards, he was questioned about these activities by his superiors, who ordered him to provide a written explanation of why he had assisted a foreign human rights group.

Mr. Cimanga was also evicted from the house to which his job as a public prosecutor entitles him.

LT. PIERRE IKOMO BAMALA KILLED

Lt. Pierre Ikomo Bamala, a 32-year-old military judge, was assassinated in his home in the Barumbu district of Kinshasa on June 2, 1993 by a group of soldiers of the Zairian Armed Forces (ZAF). Zaire's transition to democratic rule has been stymied by the refusal of President Sese Seko Mobutu to accept the legitimacy of the sovereign government of Prime Minister Etienne Tshisekedi . The ZAF remains loyal to Mobutu, and has often been used to attack and harass his opponents.

Judge Ikomo had been in charge of investigating allegations against members of the ZAF implicated in criminal activity and assaults on civilians. His murder came shortly after he had handed down guilty verdicts against a number of soldiers. Some of the soldiers allegedly involved in Judge Ikomo's murder have been arrested; others remain at large. Human rights advocates in Zaire believe that the intellectual author of the killing was a Captain Mompolo of the ZAF, who was initially arrested but not interrogated and released without charge. Zairian human rights groups report that Judge Ikomo's murder has deterred other judges from taking on sensitive cases involving the military.

After Judge Ikomo's death, his family approached the Zairian Association for Human Rights for help in bringing charges against members of the ZAF. The family then began to receive anonymous death threats. Fearing for their lives, they have ceased to pursue the case actively.

MBAYABU KANYAMA ARRESTED

Mbayabu Kanyama, an attorney from the town of Kolwezi who is affiliated with the Human Rights League of Katanga, was arrested in March 1993 after assisting a visiting US journalist investigating a wave of attacks on inhabitants of the Kasai region of Zaire. Mr. Mbayabu was flown to Lubumbashi, where he was interrogated and eventually released without charge. Fearing for his safety, Mr. Mbayabu fled with his family to the capital, Kinshasa, where he now resides.

JUSTICE NGOMA KINKEKA MASALA
JUSTICE MUNONA NTAMBANZILANJI
JUSTICE KABAMBA PENGE HARASSED, THREATENED

These three Supreme Court Justices have been harassed in response to their controversial ruling in a case involving the constitutional rights of Jehovah's Witnesses (see above, Justice Balanda Mikwin Leliel). For several months after their February 1993 decision, the judges were followed by plainclothes police and received verbal death threats and menacing remarks. During this period, they went into hiding each night.

JUSTICE LUMENGU MINTOBUS SUSPENDED

Judge Lumengu Mintobus, 50, is Chief Public Prosecutor (*Avocat Général*) at the Kinshasa/Gombe Court of Appeals. He was suspended from his judicial duties in May 1993 for allowing Olenga Nkoy, an opponent of President Mobutu, to go free. After Justice Lumengu's suspension, Mr. Olenga was given a two-month prison sentence by the judge who replaced him. After the prisoner's release, Justice Lumengu's suspension was lifted and no further charges were pressed against him.

JUDGE TSHIKANGU MUKABA ATTACKED

On August 3, 1993, Judge Tshikangu Mukaba was attacked and badly beaten by a group of plainclothes police. Members of his family were also attacked by a group of seven armed and hooded assailants who said they were looking for Judge Mukaba and intended to kill him. These attacks on the judge and his family are reportedly due to his support for Zaire's new constitution under the government of Prime Minister Tsishekedi.

JUSTICE TUKA SUSPENDED

Justice Tuka (whose full name is unknown to the Lawyers Committee) is President of the Court of General Jurisdiction (*Tribunal de Grande Instance*) in Kinshasa. He was suspended from his judicial duties in 1993 for refusing to extend a preventive detention order that had been issued against a number of journalists arrested for political reasons. Justice Tuka had also incurred the anger of pro-Mobutu forces by releasing a number of trade unionists detained in the Central Prison of Makala, Kinshasa.

JUSTICE ZOZO HARASSED

In December 1993, Ms. Zozo, a member of the Community Court (*Tribunal de la Paix*) whose full name is unknown to the Lawyers Committee, complained of threats from "the hierarchy" after she had declined to uphold a detention order against a businessman who had expressed his opposition to the Mobutu government. The defendant in the case was not the subject of criminal charges but merely of a civil complaint brought by political advisers to President Mobutu.

ASIA

Twelve Burmese lawyers are known to be serving long-term prison sentences, imposed since the ruling State Law and Order Ruling Council (SLORC) seized power in 1988. The Lawyers Committee has received new information about four of these prisoners since publishing the 1992 edition of *In Defense of Rights*.

BAWK LA IMPRISONED

Bawk La, a 43-year-old lawyer, Baptist preacher and member of the National League for Democracy (NLD), was arrested in October 1988 at the local NLD office in Myitkyina, Kachin State. He was charged retroactively with violating Order No. 2/88, which bans gatherings of more than five people, and for organizing demonstrations. He was a member of the Lawyers Committee established in Rangoon at the beginning of the pro-democracy movement in 1988. Although Bawk La's sentence should have ended in 1992, he reportedly remains in prison.

NAY MIN IMPRISONED

Nay Min, a 45-year-old lawyer who had practiced in Rangoon since 1975, was arrested on October 21, 1988 for providing information to the British Broadcasting Corporation. He was initially held under the 1975 State Protection Law, which provides for detention without charge or trial. During a year in pre-trial detention, Nay Min was subjected to electric shock torture, severe beatings and near-suffocation. On October 5, 1989, Military Tribunal No. 2

convicted him under sections 5(e) and 5(j) of the 1950 Emergency Provisions Act, for "spreading false news and rumors to fan further disturbances" and for "possession of anti-government literature which he planned to send to the BBC." He was sentenced to 14 years hard labor. However, as part of a general amnesty in November 1992, his sentence was reduced to ten years. In March 1993 two former U.S. congressmen met briefly with Nay Min and reported that he was well. As of August 1993, he was allowed to meet with family members for fifteen minutes every two weeks. He reportedly spends his time in prison medidating, praying and exercising.

SHWE OHN IMPRISONED

Shwe Ohn, a 71-year-old lawyer from Shan State, was arrested in December 1992 for writing and distributing an essay that questioned the army's role in Burmese politics and called for a transition to civilian rule that would bring the elected NLD to power. He was sentenced to one year in prison in February 1993.

U THEIN THAN OO IMPRISONED

U Thein Than Oo, a 42-year-old lawyer from Mandalay who was Joint General Secretary of the National Political Front (one of the parties banned from competing in the 1990 elections) was arrested in June 1990 for alleged underground contacts with the Communist Party of Burma (CPB). He was given a 14-year sentence, and was held at first in Mandalay prison, where he was kept in solitary confinement and severely tortured. He is now believed to be held under a forced labor regime at Obo Camp.

OTHER IMPRISONED BURMESE LAWYERS

The following cases were described in detail in the 1992 edition of *In Defense of Rights*. No further information is available on them, but all are still believed to be in detention.

GAM SENG — Secretary of opposition Democracy Action Committee; arrested October 1988, sentenced to five years.

HTUN OO — Arrested early 1989; sentenced to 20 years for "distributing leaflets of an underground organization."

KHIN AUNG — Arrested July 1991; sentence unknown.

KHIN MAUNG THAN — Arrested in 1989; charged with having contact with the underground BCP and with "distributing anti-government pamphlets"; sentence unknown.

NAI NGWE YA — Arrested December 1991; sentence unknown.

SEIN NYO TUN

Arrested late 1990; charged with having contact with the underground BCP; sentence unknown.

WIN HLAING

Arrested October 1990; sentenced to seven or ten years under the 1950 Emergency Provisions Act.

YAN AUNG

Arrested late 1990; sentenced to 10 years under the 1950 Emergency Provisions Act.

CHINA

LI GUOPING — LICENSE REVOKED

As reported in last year's edition of *In Defense of Rights*, Li Guoping had her license to practice law revoked and confiscated by the Shanghai Judicial Department on February 28, 1992. Li had written an article for a Hong Kong newspaper calling for the release from detention of her husband, Yang Zhou, who was arrested for his alleged participation in a Shanghai human rights group. She had also requested an interview with the Public Security Bureau (PSB) to discuss Yang's case. In revoking Li's license, the authorities told her that she had "used deceit" in failing to inform the PSB of her relationship to Yang until the interview was over. Throughout 1993, Li appealed to have her license to practice law restored, most recently to the Intermediate People's Court in Xuhui district, Shanghai. Her appeals have been repeatedly denied.

LU ZHIGANG INDICTED

Lu Zhigang, an undergraduate law student at Beijing University, was arrested sometime in mid-1992. According to Asia Watch, Lu was indicted by the Beijing Municipal Procuracy in September 1993 on charges of "organizing and leading a counterrevolutionary group" and carrying out "counterrevolutionary propaganda and incitement." The authorities additionally named Lu as a "chief conspirator" in a counterrevolutionary group. As of March 1993, Lu was held in Pinggu County jail, but six months later he was transferred to Beijing's Banbuqiao detention center to await trial.

REN JUN DISAPPEARED

Ren Jun, a lawyer and former student at Beijing University, disappeared. in 1993. According to the New York City-based Human Rights in China, Ren may have been one of a number of people detained by Chinese authorities who were associated with the law faculty at Beijing University. These detainees include Lu Zhigang (see above),.

WANG TIANCHENG INDICTED

As the 1992 edition of *In Defense of Rights* reported, 30-year-old Wang Tiancheng was arrested in Beijing on November 2, 1992. Wang was a law lecturer at Beijing University and editor of the college journal *Zhong-Wai Fa Xue (Chinese and Foreign Jurisprudence)*. There are unconfirmed reports that as many as seven students at the law faculty were arrested at the same time as Wang, but university officials have denied all knowledge of these cases. Wang Tiancheng is alleged by the authorities to have been a leader of two underground political groups, the Young Marxism Party and the Democratic Freedom Party. In September 1993, he was indicted on charges of "actively participating in a counterrevolutionary group" and carrying out "counterrevolutionary propaganda and incitement." As of December 31, 1993, he was still awaiting trial. If convicted, Wang could face a minimum sentence of ten years.

YU HAOCHENG HARASSED, TRAVEL DENIED

LAWYER-TO-LAWYER NETWORK
APPEAL, OCTOBER 1993

Yu Haocheng, an internationally reputed legal scholar in his late 60s, has been repeatedly refused a passport and denied permission to travel abroad. After the June 1989 crackdown on the democracy movement in Tiananmen Square, Professor Yu was detained for eighteen months and denounced by Beijing Mayor Chen Xitong as one of seventeen "bourgeois liberal intellectuals" responsible for "plotting and instigating the counterrevolutionary rebellion." After his release in December 1990, Yu continued to speak out for human rights and democratic reform in China.

In the last two years, Professor Yu has been denied permission to travel abroad eight times. Most recently, in October 1993, he was prevented from attending a seminar on human rights at the Chinese University of Hong Kong. His paper, "Human Rights and their Guarantee by Law," was delivered in absentia. The Beijing Public Security Bureau gave no reason for denying his request. Earlier, in July 1993, Professor Yu was denied permission to travel to the United States as a visiting scholar at a leading American university.

In addition to these travel bans, Yu has been subject to petty harassment by the Chinese authorities. His name has been removed from the *Who's Who of Social Scientists in China*, and the Chinese Law Society and Chinese Society of Political Science have both canceled his membership. Professor Yu has been barred from delivering papers at academic conferences, and after he wrote an article for *Future and Development* in December 1992, the magazine was closed down.

YUAN HONGBING HARASSED, TRAVEL DENIED

Yuan Hongbing, Assistant Professor of law at Beijing University and Director of the Sub-Department of Procedural Law, has faced continuous acts of harassment as a result of his alleged democracy activism in 1989. After the suppression of the movement on June 4, 1989, Yuan was accused of being "one of the chief advocates of bourgeois liberalization in China" and suspended from teaching duties from October 1989 until March 1993. University administrators also denied him the apartment to which his job entitled him, and refused his request to travel to Australia as a visiting scholar. The Communist Party Committee at Beijing University also barred Yuan from travelling to Hong Kong to teach a short course on Chinese law.

To call attention to this pattern of harassment, Yuan staged a sit-in in his office on campus on November 17, 1993. Police vans and motorcycles took up positions outside the law faculty during the sit-in, while PSB agents, armed police and campus security personnel entered the building. After this incident, Yuan reported being followed for several weeks. He remains uncertain of his future security as a law professor.

ZHOU GUOQIANG HARASSED

Thirty-nine-year-old Zhou Guoqiang, a lawyer who reportedly specializes in "impossible causes," was interrogated by the PSB on a number of occasions in 1993 and was once placed under house arrest. Zhou was instrumental in former the Beijing Workers Autonomous Federation (BWAF) during the 1989 democracy movement. Arrested in July 1989, Zhou was eventually released without charge on January 10, 1990. In August 1993, he represented BWAF leader Han Dongfang, who was forcibly returned to Hong Kong while attempting to enter China after a stay in the United States. With Zhou as counsel, Han brought an unsuccessful lawsuit against the Ministry of Public Security for cancelling his Chinese passport. In April 1993, Zhou Guoqiang provided legal services to a group of taxi drivers protesting their working conditions. As a result, he was detained on April 10 and interrogated for four hours. In early May, Zhou was placed under house arrest for sixteen hours after attempting to organize an unauthorized celebration of May 1, International Labor Day.

MARTIN LEE HARASSED

Martin Lee, a barrister and Queen's Council, is one of the the best known lawyers in Hong Kong. Leader of the United Democrats of Hong Kong (UDHK) and a member of the territory's legislative council (LEGCO), he has frequently been labelled a "subversive" by the Beijing authorities for his aggressive advocacy of democratic reform and human rights in Hong Kong. In 1993, Mr. Lee became involved in a legal dispute with Simon Li, a former judge on the Hong Kong Court of Appeal and vice-chairman of the Chinese-appointed Preparatory Committee Working Group, which is deliberating on Hong Kong's future after its reversion to Chinese sovereignty in 1997. In mid-July 1993, Mr. Li stated in Beijing that Mr. Lee and his fellow LEGCO member Szeto Wah were unfit to remain in the legislature because they had urged a run on Chinese banks after the violent suppression of the Tiananmen Square democracy movement in 1989. Mr. Lee and Mr. Wah responded that they had in fact urged the opposite and instituted legal proceedings against Mr. Li for defamation.

A leading Hong Kong firm of solicitors, Deacons, filed the original court papers on behalf of Mr. Lee and Mr. Wah, but then withdrew from the case without public explanation. Mr. Lee was then turned down by no fewer than 18 firms before he found one willing to accept the case. The Law Society of Hong Kong declined to take action, and chairman Roderick Woo remarked that: "Obviously, there would be some cases lawyers do not want to take on because there is a political ingredient to them."

The case was broadly viewed in Hong Kong, however, as an early example of the chilling effect of Beijing's political influence over the local legal profession. The influential *Far Eastern Economic Review* commented that: "This is a tale of lawyers refusing a case that might offend Peking (sic) because it pitted plaintiffs with the wrong politics against a defendant with the right connections....[The] rule of law—clearly stated rights, sensible rules and independent judges—counts for nothing if litigants cannot find lawyers willing to go to court." A public opinion poll published in Hong Kong's *Sunday Morning Post* after Mr. Lee's experience found that while 63% of respondents believed the territory now had a fair legal system, only 23% thought it would be possible to win a lawsuit against the government after 1997.

INDIA

MOHINDER SINGH GREWAL — DETAINED, HARASSED, ATTACKED

Mohinder Singh Grewal, a prominent human rights activist, is the Secretary General of the International Human Rights Organization (IHRO) of Punjab and one of the first Punjabi lawyers to investigate criminal activities by the local police. He is also well-known as co-counsel in the case of Sukhminder Singh Sandhu and Ranjit Singh Gill, Sikhs who have been incarcerated in the United States for more than six years without charge and face extradition proceedings. After assisting U.S. attorneys defending Sukhmider

Singh and Ranjit Singh, he was detained and interrogated by Indian security forces for several days. On March 21, 1993, security forces first detained Mohinder Singh's 74-year-old father and refused to release him until Mohinder Singh presented himself for interrogation. Upon arrival at the police station on March 22, Mohinder Singh was detained and questioned about his human rights activities for three days. During his detention, he was manhandled, struck about the head and threatened with torture. His apartment was also searched and his address book taken. On March 24, an Intelligence Bureau team also interrogated him for more than four hours, asking questions about the IHRO's network of contacts inside India and abroad.

KULWANT SINGH SAINI DISAPPEARED

LAWYER-TO-LAWYER NETWORK
APPEAL, MARCH 1993

Kulwant Singh Saini, 34, an attorney in Ropar, Punjab, has been missing since January 25, 1993, together with his wife Amarjit Kaur and their eighteen-month-old son Karnbir. The family has not been seen since they drove to the Ropar police station that evening, and all three are presumed dead. Kulwant Singh had been providing legal aid to Sikh political activists and Khalistan activists. The Punjab police reported that Kulwant Singh's car had been found in an irrigation canal and announced that the lawyer and his family had been murdered by two Sikh militants, who subsequently committed suicide.

The implausibility and inconsistencies in the police report led to the widespread belief in the local legal community that the police themselves were involved in the murders. The Armed Forces

(Punjab and Chandigarh) Special Powers Act of 1983 and the Punjab Disturbed Areas Act of 1983 both grant the army, paramilitary groups and police wide discretion in the use of lethal force. On March 2, 1993, more than 2,000 lawyers, including the President of the Punjab and Haryana High Court Bar Association, held a rally to press for an independent investigation. On December 2 the Supreme Court of India ordered the Central Bureau of Investigation to conduct an inquiry into the disappearance of Kulwant Singh and his family. A summary of the inquiry's findings was expected to be made public on March 31, 1994.

JAI SUDHARASAN — ARRESTED

Jai Sudharasan, a lawyer practicing in the Madras High Court, has been arrested several times over the last five years. Mr. Sudharasan provides legal assistance to traditionally underprivileged and underrepresented groups in Indian society. He has been the victim of repeated acts of harassment by the police and other government agencies. His home and office have been raided both by tax officials and by officers of India's Central Bureau of Investigation. Mr. Sudharasan was last arrested in May 1993, but was released without charges.

INDONESIA

AHMAD JAUHARI — DETAINED, THREATENED
DEDI EKADIBRATA

Ahmad Jauhari is a 28-year-old lawyer working for the Ampera Legal

Aid Institute (LBH-Ampera) in Bogor, West Java. On September 24, 1993, he was detained and interrogated by the Bogor authorities for three days. He was questioned about his involvement in a longstanding land dispute, in which local farmers in Bogor have been seeking adequate compensation for lands appropriated by developers. Dedi Ekadibrata, a 30-year-old paralegal with LBH-Ampera, was detained at the same time. He had also been providing the Bogor farmers with legal advice in connection with the land dispute. After being interrogated for several hours about his participation in demonstrations by farmers from the Ciawi District of Bogor Regency, Mr. Dedi was released without charges.

Both Mr. Ahmad and Mr. Dedi have suffered other threats and harassment as a result of their human rights advocacy in Bogor. On October 6, 1993, two weeks after his detention, ten men broke into Mr. Ahmad's house and vandalized it. His wife and newborn baby were at home at the time but were unharmed. Shortly after this attack, Mr. Ahmad received a note threatening his life and the lives of his wife and child.

DADANG TRISASONGKO HARASSED

The 1992 edition of *In Defense of Rights* reported the arrest on October 19, 1992 of Dadang Trisasongko, a human rights lawyer with the Indonesian Legal Aid Institute (*Lembaga Bantuan Hukum*, or LBH). The authorities in Surabaya, East Java charged Mr. Dadang with subversion, "incitement" and "expressing hostility toward the government." According to Maj. Gen. Hartono, military commander of East Java, Mr. Dadang was arrested because of his representation of members of the community of Singosari-Gresik, near Surabaya. The community had been involved in a dispute with the National Electricity Company (PLN), which was building high-tension power lines over local homes.

While Mr. Dadang was released after four days, and the charge of subversion dropped, the remaining charges were only "unofficially" dropped early in 1993. This means that the Indonesian authorities can reactivate these charges, which carry prison terms of up to six and seven years respectively, if Mr. Dadang should engage in any renewed human rights advocacy or representation of controversial clients. According to LBH, this "unofficial" dropping of charges is an increasingly common tactic to harass Indonesian activists.

JUDGE LINTONG OLOAN SIAHAAN HARASSED

In January 1993, Judge Lintong Oloan Siahaan, Chief Judge of the State Administrative Court in Medan, issued a restraining order against the local military commander. This was designed to prevent the commander from intervening in the leadership controversy in the Batak Protestant Christian Church (see case of Sabam Siburiam, below). The commander publicly criticized Judge Lintong's decision, and shortly thereafter the judge's home was vandalized. A few days later, Judge Lintong was ordered to leave Medan to attend a two-week legal workshop. While he was gone, his deputy vacated the restraining order against the military commander.

SABAM SIBURIAM ASSAULTED

Sabam Siburiam, a lawyer in Medan and dean of the law faculty at Nommensen University in North Sumatra province, is a defense attorney in one of the many cases involving the Batak Protestant Christian Church. (The *Huria Kristen Batak Protestan*, or HKBP, is challenging the military's intervention in the re-election of its *ephorus*, or archbishop, the Rev. Dr. S.A.E. Nababan.)

In December 1993, four unidentified men on motorcycles assaulted Mr. Sabam while he was at a roadside station changing a flat tire. He was hit repeatedly with the blunt end of a machete, and suffered deep cuts to his arm and fingers while trying to ward off the blows. He was unconscious for two-and-a-half days and hospitalized for almost a month. Mr. Sabam has stopped work on the HKBP case because of continued ill-health and fears for his safety. He has asked the police to investigate the attack, but has received no response.

MALAYSIA

CECIL RAJENDRA — TRAVEL DENIED

Cecil Rajendra is a Malaysian lawyer who provides legal aid to the rural and urban poor in Penang and Province Wellesley. He is well known as a human rights activist and environmentalist, and is a distinguished poet. On July 5, 1993, Malaysia's Ministry of Home Affairs confiscated his passport, preventing him from travelling to read his poetry in London and Vienna. The Malaysian authorities at first claimed that the Official Secrets Act prohibited them from disclosing the reasons for taking action against Mr. Rajendra. Ten days later, however, they announced that the travel ban was the result of his "anti-logging activities." Mr. Rajendra's passport was returned to him in late August 1993, but the Ministry of Home Affairs says that the case against him is still under investigation.

PAKISTAN

MIAN RIAZ QAMAR ASSAULTED

Attorney Mian Riaz Qamar was attacked by two unknown people while he slept at home in Harunabad on May 19, 1993. His assailants struck him about the head and hands with a club, breaking two fingers. Mr. Riaz is a prominent advocate for Ahmadi clients. Under Ordinance No. XX of 1984, issued by the military government of Gen. Mohammed Zia ul-Haq while the Pakistani Constitution was suspended, members of the Ahmadi community are prohibited from engaging in various religious practices and from using certain Islamic terms and symbols. The ordinance prescribes punishment for any Ahmadi who "in any manner whatsoever outrages the religious feelings of Muslims." On July 3, 1993, the Supreme Court of Pakistan dismissed eight separate appeals by Ahmadis challenging the constitutionality of Ordinance No. XX.

The police conducted an investigation into the attack on Mian Riaz Qamar, but failed to apprehend anyone. The Harunabad Bar Association carried out a boycott of the courts in protest against the assault on Mr. Riaz.

SINGAPORE

GOLPAN NAIR LICENSE SUSPENDED

Golpan Nair, a 42-year-old lawyer and one-time parliamentary candidate for the Workers' Party, was found guilty on September 23, 1992 of "serious misconduct" for allegedly attempting to discredit former Attorney General Tan Boon Telk. (See *In Defense of Rights*, 1992 edition.) Mr. Nair had already left the country for the United States, and the court sentenced him in absentia to two years' suspension from practice. It also ordered him to pay all court costs.

Mr. Nair's license to practice law is due to be reinstated in September 1994. Since his trial, however, new laws have been enacted in Singapore that allow for the suspension of a law license for up to five years. Under this new law, the Singapore government would be able to review Mr. Nair's case at any time before September 1994 and extend his period of suspension. In late 1993, the Singapore government sent Mr. Nair a bankruptcy notice on the basis of unpaid court costs of approximately US$100,000. Fearful of returning to Singapore, Mr. Nair has applied for asylum in the United States.

SOUTH KOREA

CHO GUK — INDICTED

On June 23, 1993, police arrested Cho Guk, a 29-year-old law professor at Ulsan University and a noted legal scholar. He was charged under Article 3 of the National Security Law with being a founder and member of the Korean Social Science Academy, which is considered to be an arm of the "anti-state" organization *Sanomaeng* (Socialist Workers League). A warrant for Professor

Cho Guk's arrest was not issued until two days after he was apprehended.

Professor Cho Guk was held by the police for almost three weeks and then transferred to the prosecution, where he was questioned further. In April 1992, Korea's Constitutional Court ruled that prisoners arrested under the National Security Law may be held for up to fifty days before being charged if they are suspected of such serious offenses as membership of an "anti-state" organization. Professor Cho Guk may face a lengthy prison term, or even the death penalty, for his alleged "anti-state" activities, a charge often brought to curtail the activities of leftist organizations viewed as excessively sympathetic to the Democratic People's Republic of Korea. Since 1990, numerous members of *Sanomaeng* have been arrested and imprisoned, and several of its leaders are serving life sentences. Professor Cho Guk remained in pre-trial detention at the end of 1993.

YONG WHAN CHO
BAIK SEUNG-HUN ASSAULTED, HARASSED

On July 15, 1993, lawyers Yong Whan Cho and Baik Seung-Hun were physically assaulted and verbally abused by Security Division officers of the National Police Administration. Mr. Yong had been meeting with a client, human rights activist Noh Tae-hun, when two policemen entered the office and attempted to arrest Mr. Noh for alleged offenses against the National Security Law. When the officers presented only the photocopy of an arrest warrant, Mr. Yong objected to the procedure. Shortly thereafter, another five policemen burst into the office and tried to take Mr. Noh away. When Mr. Yong again insisted on seeing a proper warrant, the agents began cursing and threatening the two lawyers, and shoved them against the wall. They then handcuffed Mr. Noh and took him away. After the incident, Mr. Yong reported that he "felt physical pain in every part of [his] body." The two lawyers filed criminal charges against the police in the Seoul District Prosecutor's office, but the prosecutor declined to take the case, ruling that the police actions did not constitute an offense.

SRI LANKA

ANONYMOUS LAWYER THREATENED

A lawyer who wishes to remain anonymous has fled Sri Lanka after receiving death threats as a result of his involvement in the Embilipitiya Central School case, in which 31 high school-age students disappeared. Several army officers, together with the principal of the Central School and his son, were allegedly involved in the boys' 1989 abduction. Working on behalf of the families of some of the missing students, the attorney began receiving death threats in late 1992, after he supported in the Appeal Court the first few applications for writs of habeas corpus on behalf of the missing students. In June 1993 he was given an ultimatum, and warned that he would be "dealt with" if he failed to undo the damage by withdrawing the applications that were pending before the court. Shortly thereafter the lawyer fled the country, fearing for his life.

M.S. PREMARATNE ASSAULTED

Despite occurring outside of the 1993 reporting period, this attack is included here because of its direct relationship to the preceding case. While no formal action has been taken against any of the suspects in the Embilipitiya Central School case, the recent discovery of a mass grave in Embilipitiya, in the Ratnapura district of southern Sri Lanka, offers persuasive evidence that the boys were in fact murdered. M.S. Premaratne was the first attorney to report the discovery of the graves to the Embilipitiya Magistrate on January 3, 1994. He was also present at the inquiry where the skeletal remains were exhibited at the Magistrate's Court on January 10. Returning home from the hearing, Mr. Premaratne was followed by a white van. When he and his driver were stopped at a roadside fruitstand, one of the four men in the van fired on Mr. Premaratne's car. The windshield was shattered, but no one was injured. The assailants fled and have not been apprehended.

WEERASENA RANAHEWA THREATENED

Attorney Weerasena Ranahewa had been representing an 11-year-old girl who was allegedly raped by a retired high-ranking police officer. After agreeing to take the case, Mr. Ranahewa received a number of death threats, as well as a threat to harm his son. In early October 1993, after the threat to his son, Mr. Ranahewa decided to withdraw from the case. The London *Times* reported that Mr. Ranahewa recognized his action was unfair to the girl in the case, but felt he was left with no alternative. In the interim, Sri Lankan Attorney General Tilak Marapana decided to drop the case against the ex-police officer.

EUROPE

VELIMIR ZEČEVIĆ
JOVAN PEJOVIĆ ASSAULTED, INDICTED
MILENKO RELJIĆ SENTENCED

Seventy-four-year-old Velimir Zečević, a retired judge of ethnic Serbian origin who had served both as a municipal court judge and a district court judge in Dubrovnik, was arrested in Zagreb in December 1992. In the course of his arrest he was beaten about the head by police. Mr. Zečević was charged on December 12, 1992 with undermining the territorial integrity of the Republic of Croatia, under Article 236 (b) of the Croatian Criminal Code. According to Amnesty International, the charges appeared to relate to a series of meetings in 1990-1992, during which Mr. Zečević and others had opposed Croatia's declaration of independence and sought to maintain the unity of the Federal Republic of Yugoslavia. They had also discussed the evacuation of the Serbian population of Dubrovnik. Thirteen other people were charged in absentia at the same time as Mr. Zečević, including lawyers Jovan Pejović and Milenko Reljić.

The case against Velimir Zečević and his co-defendants was brought before a military court. As a result of legal changes decreed by Croatian President Franjo Tudjman, these courts have assumed jurisdiction over civilians in cases involving offenses "from the military sphere." For more than two weeks after being charged, Mr. Zečević was not given a copy of the indictment, in contravention of national and international law, including Article 14 (3) of the International Covenant on Civil and Political Rights (ICCPR).

On April 13, Mr. Zečević was found not guilty of the charge and released. A portion of the trial was attended by an observer from Amnesty International. Also acquitted was lawyer Jovan Pejović, who was tried in absentia. Eleven other defendants, including lawyer Milenko Reljić, were convicted in absentia and all sentenced to prison terms of between two and ten years.

TAJIKISTAN

OYNIKHOL BOBONAZAROVA — **DETAINED**
NAZRISHOV UBAIDOV — **CLIENT ACCESS DENIED**

Oynikhol Bobonazarova was detained by Tajik police on October 8, 1993. She was subsequently charged with "organizing activities especially dangerous to the state," in violation of Article 69 of the Criminal Code, and with treason, in violation of Article 61. Ms. Bobonazarova, 46, has been dean of the Law Faculty of Tajikistan State University since 1989, where she specializes in the theory of law and the state. In bringing charges against her, the Procuracy cited Ms. Bobonazarova's membership of the banned National Salvation Front, for which she reportedly worked on refugee issues. Prior to her detention, Ms. Bobonazarova had been questioned on a number of occasions by members of the Procurator's office and by the Tajik intelligence service (KNB). She was also formerly a prominent member of the Democratic Party of Tajikistan (DPT), which shared power in a coalition government until November 1992.

Ms. Bobonazarova's lawyer, Nazrishov Ubaidov, was not allowed to see his client for a week after her arrest. After this first meeting, no further sessions were permitted. Under Tajik government regulations, a lawyer must seek permission for each meeting with a client from the investigating prosecutor in charge of the case. After his initial meeting with Ms. Bobonazarova, Mr. Ubaidov was unable to get permission for any further access to his client. Ms. Bobonazarova was released from detention in the first week of November, 1993, but remained under investigation and under house arrest in the capital city, Dushanbe.

TURKEY

SABAHATTİN ACAR
TAHİR ELÇİ INDICTED, TORTURED

LAWYER-TO-LAWYER NETWORK
APPEAL, FEBRUARY 1994

MESUT BEŞTAŞ
VEDAT ERTEN
SELİM KURBANOĞLU
HÜSNİYE ÖLMEZ
ARZU ŞAHİN
İMAM ŞAHİN INDICTED

Virtually every member of the legal profession in the city of Diyarbakır in southeastern Turkey was the victim of some form of legal or extra-judicial action by Turkish authorities during 1993. The most dramatic instance of this was an apparently concerted sweep by Turkish security forces in November and December 1993. This mass roundup of Diyarbakır lawyers resulted in charges being brought against sixteen individuals, and arrest warrants being issued for another eleven who went into hiding out of fear for their safety. All of these lawyers had acted as defense counsel in political trials before the Diyarbakır State Security Court, notably those involving defendants charged with membership in the outlawed Kurdish Workers Party (PKK). Many of the lawyers arrested were also members of Turkey's distinguished non-governmental Human Rights Association (HRA).

The clampdown on the legal profession in Diyarbakır is part of the Turkish government's drive to eradicate the PKK, which has been fighting since 1984 for Kurdish autonomy. Armed activity by PKK guerrillas has grown steadily over the last decade, with a corresponding increase in repressive actions by government forces. More than 10,000 people have died in a conflict marked by massive violations of human rights by both sides. In July 1993, the Turkish government declared all-out war against the Kurdish insurgency in the southeast, where ten provinces have been under emergency rule since Martial Law was lifted in 1987. The Emergency Legislation Governor in Diyarbakır also enjoys additional authority over another three provinces. Hundreds of Kurds have been brought before State Security Courts in Diyarbakır and elsewhere charged with membership, or support, of the PKK, and the courts have made extensive use of the death penalty.

The detainees were held under emergency legislation that allows for incommunicado detention of up to 30 days. Two of the lawyers, Sabahattin Acar and Tahir Elçi, gave Amnesty International credible accounts of torture during their period of detention in the Diyarbakır Gendarmerie Headquarters. (The Gendarmerie — soldiers who carry out police duties in rural areas under the authority of the Interior

Ministry — has no authority to interrogate lawyers. Under Turkey's Law No.1136, the Law Relating to Lawyers, such interrogation may be carried out either by the Public Prosecutor or by police acting under the authorization of the Justice Minister, depending on the nature of the alleged offense.) Torture appears to be a commonplace occurence in Turkish police facilities and detention centers. As the European Committee for the Prevention of Torture (ECPT) reported after inspecting Turkish facilities in 1990, 1991 and 1992: "In light of all the information at its disposal, the ECPT can only conclude that the practice of torture and other forms of severe ill-treatment of persons in police custody remains widespread in Turkey and that such methods are applied to both ordinary and criminal suspects and persons held under anti-terrorism provisions."

Sabahattin Acar reported that during his interrogation on November 18 he was "tortured in a degrading manner," and stripped naked while agents asked him to name the foreign organizations to whom he had faxed information about human rights abuses. Soldiers loaded their weapons and threatened to take him out of Diyarbakır and kill him. On hearing the sound of his colleagues being tortured, Mr. Acar signed a statement while still blindfolded.

Tahir Elçi was detained at his office on November 23 by police who seized files from more than 100 cases in which he was involved. According to Amnesty International, Mr. Elçi was taken blindfolded to Cizre Police Headquarters and confronted with documents he had produced on human rights abuses, including submissions to the European Human Rights Commission of the Council of Europe. He was stripped naked by agents who beat him, squeezed his testicles and showered him with verbal abuse. He was then transferred to the

Diyarbakır Gendarmerie Intelligence Interrogation Center where he was again beaten and subjected to mock execution.

The eight lawyers named above remained in custody in Diyarbakır at the end of 1993, charged under Article 168 (2) of the Turkish Penal Code, which makes it an offense to aid and abet members of an illegal armed organization. An initial hearing in the case was scheduled for February 17, 1994.

GAZANFER ABBASİOĞLU
NİYAZİ CEM
MERAL DANIŞ
FUAT HAYRİ DEMİR
BAKİ DEMİRHAN
NEVZAT KAYA
ŞİNASİ TUR INDICTED

These seven Diyarbakır lawyers were picked up by security forces in the same sweep during November and December 1993, and face the same charges as their colleagues described above. Instead of remaining in detention, however, they were released on bail on December 14, 1993, apparently in recognition of World Human Rights Day. They were also set to appear before the Diyarbakır State Security Court on February 17, 1994. This second group of detainees includes Meral Danis, secretary of the Diyarbakır branch of the HRA.

ABDULLAH AKIN
M. ARİF ALTINKALEM
SEDAT ASLANTAŞ
MEHMET BİÇEN

FERDİAN ÇELİK
ZAFER GÜR
CABBAR LEYGARA
SİNAN (OR SEZGIN) TANRIKLU
FEVZİ VEZNEDAROGLU
NİYAZİ YALÇIN
EDİP YILDIZ THREATENED

An additional eleven Diyarbakır lawyers, whose names are listed above, went into hiding on learning of the mass arrests of their colleagues. One of the fugitives, M. Arif Altinkalem, was charged in absentia under Article 168 (2) of the Penal Code. Arrest warrants were issued for the other ten, including Diyarbakır HRA official Fevzi Veznedaroglu, who was the subject of a Lawyer-to-Lawyer Network Appeal in December 1992 after receiving numerous death threats. Prior to going underground at the end of 1993, Mr. Veznedaroglu had reported receiving further anonymous telephone threats on a daily basis.

SEDAT ASLANTAŞ HARASSED

Sedat Aslantaş, a member of the management committee of the Diyarbakır branch of the HRA (see above), also faced separate charges under Article 8 (1) of Turkey's Anti-Terrorist Law. The arrest warrant against Mr. Aslantaş cited a press statement that he and 23 others had issued on May 27, 1993, complaining about the death in custody on May 20 of a villager, Kutbettin Tekin. After meeting with the prosecutor in Bismil, where the death occurred, Mr. Aslantaş and his colleagues had concluded that it was an extra-judicial killing by Turkish security forces. Bekir Selçuk, chief prosecutor for the Diyarbakır area, told a visiting delegation from the Law Society of England and Wales that he had authorized the warrant against Mr. Aslantaş because the press statement "criticizes the officials of the anti-terrorist police and because of this there is separatism in it."[1] Mr. Aslantaş told the Law Society that he believed his arrest was also motivated by his role in organizing a "peace festival" in Diyarbakır involving music, entertainment and Kurdish folk dancing. The festival was banned by Ünal Erkan, Governor of the State of Emergency Area. Together with ten other Diyarbakır lawyers, Mr. Aslantaş went into hiding at the end of 1993 (see above).

HAKKI BİNGÖL
AHMET BOZKURT ÇAĞLAR
FAİK CANDAN
AYŞENUR DEMİRKALE
CEMAL EMİR
MERYEM ERDAL
ERCAN KANAR
EREN KESKİN
AHMET KİRİMLİ
CABBAR LEYGARA
MUSTAFA OLCAYTO
HÜSNİYE ÖLMEZ

---

1. The Law Society, in conjunction with the Kurdistan Human Rights Project (KHRP), "Lawyers in Fear; Law in Jeopardy, Report of a Delegation to Istanbul and Diyarbakir in the South Eastern Region of Turkey to investigate the situation of lawyers defending people in political trials and involved in human rights work, 5-11 October, 1993," at 16-17.

HÜSNÜ ÖNDÜL
SEDAT ÖZEVİN
NUSRET ÖZTÜRK
HÜSEYİN TÜRHALLİ
ERTUGRUL USANMAZ
FEVZİ VEZNEDAROĞLU
CELAL VURAL
EDİP YİLDİZ
ALİ YİLDIRIM
SEVTAP YOKUŞ INDICTED

The 22 lawyers named above face prosecution under Article 8 of the Anti-Terrorism Law. The charges, which carry a sentence of two to five years imprisonment, stem from an April 1992 petition to the United Nations, in which the lawyers complained about the killing of more than a hundred civilians by security forces during peaceful celebrations of the Kurdish New Year (*Newroz*) in 1992. Prosecutors at the Ankara State Security Court have demanded five-year prison sentences. Seven of the 22 lawyer — Eren Keskin, Ercan Kanar, Hüsniye Ölmez, Hüseyin Türhalli, Fevzi Veznedaroglu, Edip Yıldız and Sevtap Yokuş — are simultaneously involved in other cases (see separate entries).

METİN CAN KILLED

LAWYER-TO-LAWYER NETWORK
APPEAL, FEBRUARY 1993

Metin Can, a lawyer and chairman of the Elazığ branch of the HRA, was tortured and killed sometime in late February, 1993. On February 21, Mr. Can received a telephone call from someone purporting to be a policeman, notifying him that a client had been involved in a car accident and that he should report to the police station immediately. Mr. Can contacted his friend Dr. Hasan Kaya, a physician and fellow HRA member, and the two left together in Mr. Can's car. On February 22, an unknown person telephoned Mr. Can's home and said: "We killed Metin and Hasan. Our condolences!" Mr. Can's car was found abandoned that day in Elazığ.

The two men's bodies were discovered on February 27 near the town of Tunceli, 120 kilometers away. Their hands had been tied behind their backs; their shoes were missing; their bodies were marked by cigarette burns; Dr. Kaya's eyes had been gouged out; both men had been shot once in the head, execution-style. Autopsies also revealed that Mr. Can had been strangled and had a broken rib; Dr. Kaya had a broken tooth and his neck also bore cord marks. The deaths of Mr. Can and Dr. Kaya were among the more than one thousand unsolved murders that have come to be widely known in Turkey as "unknown perpetrator killings." However, the lack of any serious investigation by the authorities, as well as the specific circumstances of Mr. Can's disappearance, raise reasonable fears of police involvement in the killings. His widow, Mrs. Fatma Can, has also received threats since his murder. Protests against the death of Metin Can also led indirectly to prosecutions, violence and acts of harassment against other Turkish lawyers, which are detailed below.

CONTEMPORARY JURISTS ASSOCIATION — ASSAULTED , DETAINED

According to Turkey's Human Rights Association (HRA), members of the İzmir branch of the HRA and the Contemporary Jurists Association were briefly detained and beaten in Aydın Prison on

May 26, 1993. The lawyers and human rights advocates were part of a delegation that had gone to Aydın to speak to prison authorities about a hunger strike underway in the facility at the time.

ŞEVKET EPOZDEMİR KILLED

Şevket Epozdemir, a lawyer and representative of the HRA in the township of Tatvan in the eastern province of Bitlis, was kidnapped by unknown persons after returning home from work on November 25, 1993. The following day his body was found in a snowdrift by the roadside approximately 20 kilometers from the town of Bitlis, where it had been abandoned. This area has been used as a dumping ground for the bodies of other victims of "unknown perpetrator killings" in eastern and southeastern Turkey. The autopsy report from Bitlis hospital indicated that Mr. Epozedemir had been tortured and then killed by a single gunshot to the head. According to members of Mr. Epozdemir's family, local authorities have made no serious effort to investigate the murder.

FUAT ERDOĞUN
ULUTAN GÜN
ÜMRAN GÜN
FETHİYE PEKŞEN
ZERRİN SARI
BEDİİ YARAYICI INDICTED, IMPRISONED

As reported in the 1992 edition of *In Defense of Rights*, these six lawyers — all members of the Istanbul Bar and associates of the People's Legal Aid Bureau (*Halkin Hukuk Bürosu*) — were indicted in November 1992 by the Chief Public Prosecutor of the Istanbul State Security Court. (For separate charges against Fethiye

Pekşen, see below.) They were charged under Article 169 of the Penal Code with "sheltering and helping" members of an illegal organization, and the prosecutor demanded prison terms of at least five years for each defendant. However, under the sentencing provisions of the 1991 Law to Fight Terrorism, these terms may be increased by 50% if guilty verdicts are returned. The indictment alleged that the six had "acted as couriers between members of an organization in prison and a person high up in that organization outside." The organization referred to in the indictment is the Revolutionary Left (*Devrimci Sol*).

The trial of the six lawyers began in early 1993, but hearings were postponed until September. Ms. Pekşen was sentenced to three years and nine months in prison, and the sentence was subsequently upheld by the Supreme Court. No details are available to the Lawyers Committee of the sentences imposed on the remaining five defendants.

SEYDİ AHMET ERİBOL
METANET ÖZTÜRK ASSAULTED, INDICTED

The Kayseri State Security Court has indicted lawyers Ahmet Eribol and Metanet Öztürk, along with five other members of the Ordu branch of the HRA—Hakki Katırcıoğlu, Atilla Cebi, Avni Kalafat, Bahattin Kılıç and Ömer Yavuz—for allegedly publishing separatist propaganda. The prosecutor has demanded a minimum sentence of two years imprisonment. Mr. Ozturk was also one of a number of people beaten by police in early 1993 when a delegation headed by HRA president Akın Birdal approached the entrance to Turkey's National Assembly building to demand an inquiry into the murder of Metin Can. (see above)

FETHİ GÜMÜŞ
HÜSEYİN TÜRHALLİ
SEVTAP YOKUŞ
SABAHATTIN ACAR INDICTED

Fethi Gümüş, chair of the Diyarbakır Bar Association, was prosecuted in two different courts in 1993 on charges arising from a statement that condemned the destruction of Kurdish villages by Turkish security forces. The statement, which was signed by 20 people in all, was read out at a press conference attended by Kurdish members of parliament. According to the Human Rights Foundation of Turkey, some 800 Kurdish villages have been destroyed in the past two years. According to the Law Society of England and Wales three other Diyarbakır lawyers — Hüseyin Türhalli, Sevtap Yokuş and Sabahattin Acar (see above) — faced the same charges. This was at least the eighth time that Mr. Gumus had been prosecuted for issuing statements critical of human rights abuses by the security forces. On one occasion, in 1984, he was detained for fifty days and tortured. All of these earlier prosecutions ended in Mr. Gümüş's acquittal.

The first of the two 1993 prosecutions, brought under Article 159 of the Turkish Penal Code ("insulting the integrity of the Turkish State"), also ended in the acquittal of all four lawyers. The second was under Article 312 of the Penal Code ("inciting people to uprising"). No information was available to the Lawyers Committee on the outcome of this case.

ULUTAN GÜN IMPRISONED

Ulutan Gün, head of the Istanbul branch of the Contemporary Jurists Association and an associate of the People's Legal Aid Bureau (*Halkin Hukuk Bürosu*), was sentenced to ten months imprisonment by Istanbul No.2 Criminal Court on September 29, 1993. He had been charged under Article 159 of the Turkish Penal Code with having "insulted the justice system" in an article published in the periodical *Mücadele* (*Struggle*). The chief editor of the periodical, Namık Kemal Cibaroğlu, was also found guilty on the same charge. Conflicting reports say that Mr. Cibaroglu was sentenced to either six or ten months in prison. The annual report, *Attacks on the Press 1993* , published by the Committee to Protect Journalists, notes that 34 of the 38 issues of *Mücadele* published in 1993 were seized by police, and that the magazine was closed down for 16 days. Mr. Gün was also one of six lawyers concurrently on trial on charges of "sheltering and helping" members of *Devrimci Sol.* (see above)

YEŞİM İSLEGAN THREATENED

Yeşim İslegan, chair of the Izmir branch of the HRA, reportedly received repeated death threats throughout 1993. Dr. Islegan was also harassed by anonymous callers who played tape recordings over his telephone that appeared to be the sounds of people being tortured.

ERCAN KANAR
ALİ RIZA DİZDAR INDICTED, THREATENED

Like many other Turkish lawyers, Ercan Kanar, vice-president of the HRA and chair of its Istanbul branch, and Ali Riza Dizdar, chair of the Contemporary Jurists Association, faced multiple charges as well as other forms of harassment during 1993.

Both men were prosecuted under Article 8 of the Anti-Terrorist Law as the result of a March 3 petition to the governor of Istanbul, in which they alleged that Metin Can and Dr. Hasan Kaya (see above) had been assassinated by security forces. Both Mr. Kanar and Mr. Dizdar were acquitted of this charge on September 30. However, separate charges were also brought against Mr. Dizdar under the Law on Associations for signing the March 3 petitition on behalf of the Contemporary Jurists Association without receiving official authorization. Under this law, the government must grant permission for a public document to be signed in the name of an association, even if the association itself has already given permission. This offense carries a fine on first conviction and a prison term on any subsequent convictions.[2]

Ercan Kanar also faces charges of "insulting the state," arising from a public statement that he made in 1992 to the effect that the Turkish authorities were "immoral" as well as "terrorist" for their conduct on human rights. In this case, the prosecution has demanded a ten-year prison sentence. Mr. Kanar is also under investigation by the Istanbul Public Prosecutor's Office in connection with two articles that he wrote for the June 25, 1993 and July 24, 1993 issues of the pro-

---

2. For further analysis of the Law on Associations, and other restrictions on freedom of association in Turkey, see Lawyers Committee for Human Rights, *Shackling the Defenders: Legal Restrictions on Independent Human Rights Advocacy Worldwide* (March 1994), at 118-121.

Kurdish newspaper *Ozgur Gundem*. If prosecuted, this case would come before the Second Severe Penalties Court of Istanbul.

In addition to these various legal proceedings, Mr. Kanar has been the target of a number of anonymous telephone threats in response to his human rights advocacy. Serious threats from the Turkish police were also relayed to Mr. Kanar through a client, Mehmet Baltaş, who was accused of aiding and abetting the PKK. While in police detention, Mr. Baltaş was subjected to "Palestinian hanging," a form of mock crucifixion. His torturers told him that his lawyer would be given the same treatment. Such threats are reportedly a common police tactic to dissuade clients from using the services of particular advocates.

EREN KESKİN THREATENED, ATTEMPTED KIDNAPPING

Eren Keskin, secretary of the Istanbul branch of the HRA, told a visiting delegation of the Law Society of England and Wales of constant death threats during 1993, as well as an attempt to kidnap her. She has received threatening phone calls both at her home and her office. The anonymous callers swear at her, threaten to kill her and even tell her the date of her impending death. Like Yesim Islegan (see above), Ms. Keskin also reported receiving anonymous phone calls that appear to be tape-recordings of people undergoing torture. Her family has also been harassed, with callers alleging that Ms. Keskin is under the direct orders of PKK leader Abdullah Öcalan and threatening to kill her. Ms. Keskin believes that these threats all emanate from the police, and that her telephone is tapped.

Police also reportedly attempted to abduct Ms. Keskin at some time in the summer of 1993 as she was entering her home with another lawyer, Ayşe Zarakol. Two men, one of whom she recognized as a member of the anti-terrorist police, were parked in a car in front of the building. As Ms. Keskin and Mr. Zarakol approached, one of the policemen got out of the car and opened the rear door. Ms. Keskin managed to run inside the house while Mr. Zarakol waved down a taxi. Shortly after the incident, an anonymous caller told Ms. Keskin, "OK, you got away this time. You will not get away next time." Ms. Keskin is fearful of going home alone and does not go out at night. She told the Law Society that she had registered no complaint with the authorities since she believes that they would never order an independent investigation of these incidents.

AHMET ZEKİ OKÇUOĞLU IMPRISONED

In February 1993, Istanbul lawyer Ahmet Zeki Okçuoğlu was convicted in the Istanbul State Security Court under Article 8 (1) of the Anti-Terrorism Law and sentenced to eighteen months imprisonment. His prosecution arose from an article he wrote on the Kurdish question in the magazine *The Democrat*. On October 6, 1993, Mr. Okçuoğlu's sentence was upheld by the Court of Appeal in Ankara. He was also disbarred, since the regulations of the Turkish Bar Association require it to disbar any member sentenced to more than one year in prison, even if the sentence is for a political offense under local laws that contravene the European Convention on Human Rights.

FETHİYE PEKŞEN IMPRISONED

Istanbul lawyer Fethiye Pekşen was detained at the end of September 1993 along with seventeen other people on charges of membership in the illegal organization *Devrimci Sol*. During her detention, she was convicted during a concurrent trial on charges of passing *Devrimci Sol* documents to inmates of the Izmir Buca Closed Prison. Ms. Pekşen was sentenced to a prison term of three years nine months.

SANAL SARUHAN ASSAULTED

In October 1993, 124 people went on trial on charges connected with violent clashes in the town of Sivas on July 2. A number of lawyers representing the families of those killed in encounters between the security forces and an illegal Islamist organization were barred from attending the hearings. In the course of an altercation between the lawyers and police blocking their access to the courtroom, policemen attacked Sanal Saruhan, chair of the Contemporary Jurists Association. According to the Human Rights Foundation of Turkey, the agents "tried to throttle" Ms. Saruhan. Although the lawyers were eventually admitted to the courtroom, the trial was further disrupted when fist-fights broke out between defense and prosecution attorneys.

SINAN (or SEZGİN) TANRIKLU INDICTED, DISCIPLINARY ACTION

Sinan (or Sezgin) Tanriklu, vice-chair of the Diyarbakır Bar Association, is one of the eleven Diyarbakır lawyers who went into hiding after warrants for their arrest were issued in December 1993. (see above) At this time, Mr. Tanriklu was also facing criminal charges and possible disciplinary proceedings arising from an earlier incident.

In May and June 1993, Mr. Tanriklu was involved in representing the *muhtar*, or village head, of Caglayan before the Diyarbakır No.1 State Security Court. The proceedings against the *muhtar* followed an earlier, unsuccessful prosecution of his son, who was acquitted after the court ruled that the statement on which his prosecution was based was unreliable. Mr. Tanriklu told a visiting delegation of the Law Society of England and Wales that the son's statement had been extracted under torture.[3]

Nonetheless, charges were then brought against the *muhtar* himself, with the only evidence against him being his son's discredited statement. Mr. Tanriklu drew the court's attention to this anomaly, and suggested that it had failed to give due weight to its own earlier finding. Lawyers in Diyarbakır have suggested that the inconsistency in the court's behavior may reflect the fact that a ceasefire between the PKK and government forces was in effect at the time of the son's acquittal; the case against the *muhtar* was opened after the ceasefire collapsed.

The court reported Mr. Tanriklu's arguments to the Ministry of Justice, which recommended that an inquiry be opened to determine whether it was appropriate for the Turkish Bar Association to take disciplinary action against Mr. Tanriklu. In addition to possible disciplinary proceedings, Mr. Tanriklu also faces criminal prosecution for contempt of court. For this offense, the potential sentence is a prison term of six months to three years.

---

3. "Lawyers in Fear; Law in Jeopardy," at 18-19.

ŞİNASI TUR DETAINED, TORTURED

Şinasi Tur, one of sixteen Diyarbakir lawyers involved in the mass arrests of November-December 1993, had also been detained on three prior occasions. In each instance, he had been tortured while in detention. The most recent episode was in January 1993, just as Mr. Tur was completing his training as a lawyer. He was detained at first for eight days and charged with harboring PKK guerrillas in his home. He alleged that he was tortured with high-pressure jets of cold water and with electric shocks to his genitals and little fingers. He was also beaten and subjected to "Palestinian hanging." As a result of this torture, he was obliged to sign a statement confessing that he had met on October 27, 1992 with a PKK guerrilla named Omar Demirel.

After a court appearance, Mr. Tur was remanded in custody in Diyarbakir Prison for a further three months. He was later released on bail, however, after the court discovered that the guerrilla, Omar Demirel, had died on October 10, 1992, and that the meeting described in the coerced confession could not therefore have taken place. Despite this development, the case against Mr. Tur has not been dismissed, and the charges may be reactivated at any time. If convicted, he could face a sentence of 15 to 22 years in prison.

NİYAZİ YALÇIN DETAINED

According to the HRA, lawyer Niyazi Yalcin, a member of the Adana Bar Association, was detained in the Doğubeyazıt district of Ağrı in mid-August 1993. No further details of this case are available.

DEFENSE SOLICITORS IN NORTHERN IRELAND THREATENED

Defense lawyers operating within the framework of emergency legislation in Northern Ireland continued to report frequent threats, including death threats, and other incidents of abuse during 1993. In its August 1993 report to the United Nations Sub-Commission on the Prevention of Discrimination and Protection of Minorities, the International Commission of Jurists reported that 39 lawyers had been subject to abuse and threats by officers of the Royal Ulster Constabulary (RUC) during the preceding 12 months. Fearing reprisals, lawyers reporting this kind of abuse have generally sought anonymity. Most of the threats by RUC officers were reportedly conveyed to clients during interrogation in the absence of their solicitors. In at least one other instance, a defense lawyer received threatening telephone calls from Loyalist paramilitaries at his home in the middle of the night after he had given a radio interview.

Solicitors have been more severely affected than barristers, and the volume of threats appears to be directly proportionate to the degree of a lawyer's involvement in the defense of clients facing charges under emergency anti-terrorism laws. Many officers of the Royal Ulster Constabulary (RUC) continue to identify lawyers with the supposed allegiances and actions of their clients, in contravention of Basic Principle 18 of the UN Basic Principles on the Role of Lawyers (see appendix).

The United Kingdom government has consistently maintained that it will not tolerate official intimidation of defense lawyers, yet has taken few steps to prevent it. Current emergency legislation continues to permit the RUC to interrogate suspects in the absence of counsel, to delay access to lawyers in 48-hour increments, and effectively to limit the right to counsel of choice. Current practice in detention centers, where most of the alleged intimidation of lawyer take place, likewise continues to permit interrogation of suspects without audio or videotape recording or any other meaningful safeguard against abuse. The government has so far refused to institute any independent inquiry either into the intimidation of lawyers or into the murder of Patrick Finucane, a prominent Belfast solicitor who was killed by loyalist paramilitaries in 1989. Officials instead continue to advise attorneys to lodge complaints with the same RUC that is the subject of many attorneys' complaints in the first place.

YUGOSLAVIA (KOSOVO)

FATLIK LILA
SOKOL DOBRUNA IMPRISONED

LAWYER-TO-LAWYER NETWORK
APPEAL, NOVEMBER 1993

Fatlik Lila and Sokol Dobruna are ethnic Albanian lawyers living in Kosovo, which has been under direct rule by Serbian authorities since 1990. (The dismissal of more than 200 ethnic Albanian lawyers and judges in Kosovo in 1990-1991 is described in the 1991 edition of *In Defense of Rights.*) Both Mr. Lila and Mr. Dobruna were involved in drafting the Constitution for an independent republic of Kosovo.

Mr. Lila was convicted in October 1992 under Article 116 of the Criminal Code of Yugoslavia with "undermining the territorial integrity of Yugoslavia." He was sentenced to five years in prison. Mr. Dobruna was convicted at the same time of "helping set up an illegal enemy organization" of ethnic Albanians and of travelling abroad to raise money for the organization. He was sentenced to six years in prison.

Mr. Lila and Mr. Dobruna appealed their convictions in October 1993, citing numerous procedural defects in their original trials and their abusive treatment in detention, in violation of both federal and international law. According to Bajram Kelmendi, attorney for the two lawyers, the issues on appeal included: the use of torture during investigation; conduct of the investigation by state security agents instead of the investigating judge, as stipulated by Serbian law; denial of the right of the accused to be present at their own trial, in contravention of Article 281 of the Federal Law on Criminal Procedure; denial of the accused's immediate right to counsel; and the denial of counsel's right to confer freely with his clients.

According to the Council for the Defense of Human Rights and Freedoms in Prishtina, the Supreme Court of Serbia heard the appeals on October 11, 1993, but has not informed the detainees or their lawyers of the outcome. Mr. Lila and Mr. Dobruna remain in detention in the prison of Dubrave.

LATIN AMERICA/ CARIBBEAN

RAUL BORRINO ATTACKED, THREATENED

In June, an unknown group of assailants fired shots at the home of Judge Raúl Borrino in a suburb of Buenos Aires. He later received telephone death threats in which he was told, "You are going to be assasinated by a police official." It is unclear whether these incidents were connected to a particular case.

BUENOS AIRES JUDICIARY THREATENED

In July 1993, the Bar Association of the City of Buenos Aires denounced a "convulsion" of threats against judges. A study completed by court officials for the Province of Buenos Aires (which comprises 42% of Argentina's population) concluded that every single member of the province's Criminal Court judiciary had received threats, along with many prosecutors and civil court judges. One judge reported that he had been followed by police intelligence units. When another judge investigated the incident, he received a bomb threat in his office. A prosecutor reported that a 9mm bullet had been suspended in a noose from his rearview mirror. According to local press reports, threats against the judiciary were so pervasive that the Supreme Court of Buenos Aires installed a fax machine for the sole purpose of receiving reports from judges throughout the province. Non-governmental legal organizations in Argentina, as well as the press, have criticized the government for failing to determine who was responsible for this wave of threats, despite indications that many of them emanated from the police or paramilitary groups. A majority of judges indicated that threats had become so commonplace it was no longer productive to report them.

LAURA INES COSIDOY ATTACKED, THREATENED

Laura Inés Cosidoy, a federal judge in the city of Rosario, was the target of numerous death threats in May and June, 1993. Members of her immediate family were also threatened. The threats appear to have been related to Judge Cosidoy's investigation of connections between Rosario police officials and a local narcotics ring. The threats began days after Judge Cosidoy had ordered the arrest of six police officers, the majority of them high-level officials. One caller identified himself as a member of "the services," and warned: "Don't get involved in this war, you have a husband and children." Another caller warned that an operative from the military dictatorship that ruled Argentina between 1976 and 1983 would "liquidate" Judge Cosidoy. Four days later, when the judge called a seventh police official to testify and then imprisoned him, her home was fired on by unidentified assailants, who fled after a shootout with the judge's police bodyguards.

Although the identity of those responsible for the threats and attacks against Judge Cosidoy was never established, the culprits are believed to belong to factions within the police and security forces. In an apparent effort by the government to defuse the situation, Judge Cosidoy was promoted to a federal appellate judgeship and relieved of her responsibilities in the investigation. An appellate court subsequently reversed Judge Cosidoy's earlier ruling that the seven police officers implicated in the case should be placed under investigative detention, and the men were released.

LUCIO DATO KILLED

Lucio Dato, Vice-President of the Bar Association of Paraná, the capital of Entre Rios province, was found murdered in his office in October 1993. Medical examiners concluded that Mr. Dato had been tortured with an electric cattle prod and that his death had resulted from internal hemorrages caused by the insertion of a stick into his rectum. At the time of his death, Mr. Dato and his partner maintained a docket of more than 800 cases on behalf of workers dismissed by the state. The judge investigating Mr. Dato's murder, Susana Medina de Rizzo (see below), received an anonymous letter indicating that the killing was politically motivated, and implicating several persons aligned with the former military dictatorship. She was later warned by an anonymous caller that she would suffer the same fate as Mr. Dato if she pursued her investigation.

ALBERTO RAMON DURAN THREATENED

In August 1993, Judge Alberto Ramón Durán of La Plata, the capital city of the Province of Buenos Aires, reported that he had received death threats. He also reported that two men had attempted to abduct his 10-year-old daughter from her fifth grade classroom on June 15, 1993. Shortly after the attempt, Judge Durán received an envelope with a threatening note and photographs of his mother, daughter and 11-year-old son, indicating that unknown persons had been following his family for months. Judge Durán had been the target of an assassination attempt in 1988 after ordering the search of a police headquarters in Lanus. He also was well known for having denied a petition by rebel military leaders known as *carapintadas* ("painted faces") held in Magdalena prison. Official investigations into the threats against

Judge Durán in 1993 failed to identify the judge's assailants, but the threats were widely believed to have been political in origin.

ENTRE RIOS PROVINCIAL JUDICIARY THREATENED

In July 1993, court officials in Entre Ríos Province announced that there had been 35 bomb threats in 60 days, the majority directed against judicial officials.

MARIA MAGDALENA GAIM THREATENED

Attorney María Magdalena Gaim filed a complaint in December 1993 alleging that she and a client had received repeated anonymous death threats. Ms. Gaim had earlier accused high-level police officials in Quilmes, on the outskirts of Buenos Aires, of torturing this client as part of an extortion scheme. The threats began after a judge investigating the case ordered a search of the police precinct and called several police officers to testify.

MIRIAM GALIZZI THREATENED

Miriam Galizzi, President of the Bar Association of Paraná, received death threats in connection with the investigation of the murder of Lucio Dato (see above).

DANIEL LLERMANOS ATTACKED

On July 18, 1993, Federal Judge Daniel Llermanos of Lomas de Zamora, on the southern outskirts of Buenos Aires, reported that a group of armed men had fired on his bodyguards in the middle of the night. Known for his investigation into several controversial environmental cases, Judge Llermanos indicated that he did not know whether the incident was related to a specific case or was simply part of a general wave of threats against judges, apparently intended to destabilize the government and discredit the judiciary. Judge Llermanos had also received threats against himself and his family in May 1992 in connection with his investigation of industries alleged to be distributing contaminated products for human consumption.

SUSANA MEDINA DE RIZZO THREATENED

Susana Medina de Rizzo, a judge in Entre Ríos Province, received repeated threats in her office and home in May and June 1993, after she charged the provincial Chief of Police with obstruction of justice in a murder investigation in which public officials had been implicated. During one incident, a caller claimed that a bomb had been planted in Judge Medina's home. The judge's neighbors also received threatening phone calls. An unknown group identifying itself as the Free Command (*Comando Libre*) claimed responsibility for the calls. Judge Medina was also threatened in connection with her investigation into the death of Paraná labor lawyer Lucio Dato (see above).

BRAZIL

FRANCIACO ABREU
JOSE DO CARMO
CELSO SAMPAIO

THREATENED

In Brazil's rural Northeast, land disputes between settlers and large landowners are among the most common sources of violence. According to Amnesty International, the Brazilian Attorney General's department investigated 173 cases of murders by hired gunmen in rural areas during 1993. Military police were proved to have been directly involved in 72 of these cases, and civilian police in another eight. It is common for landowners to acquire land through illegal deeds and titles without regard to the existing occupants, and settlers or squatters who lack official title or cannot adequately defend themselves in court are often forcibly evicted. Landowners frequently resort to violence in these conflicts, with near-total impunity. For reasons of safety and effectiveness, it has become customary for Brazilian human rights advocates to work in groups when investigating settlers' rights and land disputes. Even so, these advocates often encounter violence and threats.

On November 6, 1993, gunmen intimidated three lawyers and a number of representatives of Brazilian human rights organizations as they sought to investigate violence against settlers near Lake Santo Agostinho in the northeastern state of Maranhão. The lawyers were Franciaco Abreu of the Central Workers Union, Jose Do Carmo of the Pastoral Land Commission and Celso Sampaio of the Maranhão Society for the Defense of Human Rights.

The lawyers and human rights officials arrived at Santo Agostinho accompanied by a police officer who had been assigned to them for their protection. When the group realized that the entrance to the settlement was blocked by a tractor belonging to two local landowners, Paulo Eudes Carneiro and Emidio Jose Carneiro, as well as by several gunmen, the police officer informed the lawyers that he could no longer guarantee their safety and refused to enter the settlement. As a result, the lawyers and human rights advocates were forced to withdraw.

Investigations into the settlement began in the the spring of 1993, when a commission made up of lawyers and representatives from several local human rights organizations sought to investigate allegations of unfair treatment of settlers by landowners in the state of Maranhão. One of the commission's first cases was the Santo Agostinho settlement, where the Carneiro brothers were imposing an illegal tax on settlers farming land near the lake. The commission found that most of the settlers were afraid to denounce any wrongdoing by the Carneiro brothers as a result of death threats from gunmen hired by the Carneiro family.

On the night of their visit to Santo Agostinho, November 6, the human rights commission was again intimidated by a group of some 30 gunmen who surrounded the inn where they were sleeping in the nearby town of São Bernardo. As a result, members of the commission met on November 8 with the State Secretary of Public Security, Guilherme Ventura, and State Director of Police, Emanoel Bastos, in an effort to prevent further harassment of their investigation. The commission asserted that it would hold the Governor of Maranhão State and the Secretary of Public Security directly responsible for any future acts of violence against the settlers or representatives of the human rights organizations. It also requested that the landowners and their gunmen be disarmed.

LAVOISIER ARNOU DA SILVEIRA
MARIVALDO BASSAL FREIRE
PAULO COELHO PEREIRA
ALCI DA ROCHA
ANTONEITA MAGALHAES AGULAR
HESMONE SARAIVA GRANJEIRO THREATENED

These six lawyers were included among nine names on an anonymous death list that circulated in early 1993 in a neighborhood of the town of Boa Vista, in the northern state of Roraima. Paulo Coelho Pereira, federal counsellor for the Brazilian Bar Association (AOB) in Roraima, was shot dead on February 19, 1993 (see below). Professor Hesmone Saraiva Granjeiro is president of the AOB in Roraima.

JAYME BENVENUTO DE LIMA
VALDENIA BRITO MONTEIRO
KATIA COSTA PEREIRA
ESTERIO RAMOS GALVAO ATTACKED, THREATENED

On July 23, 1993, lawyer Jayme Benvenuto de Lima was ambushed by two unidentified persons as he drove home. While one person threatened Mr. Benvenuto de Lima with a gun, a second car drove by and one of its occupants fired shots at him. Mr. Benvenuto de Lima managed to duck the bullet and was unharmed. According to Amnesty International, Mr. Benvenuto de Lima and two colleagues, Valdenia Brito Monteiro and Katia Costa Pereira, have also received death threats as a result of their involvement in several cases against corruption within the Tribunal system of the state of Pernambuco. All three lawyers work for the *Gabinete de Apoio Juridico as Organizaçoes Populares* (GAJOP), a human rights organization that gives legal advice to disadvantaged people and community organizations in the state of Pernambuco. In addition, the General Magistrate of Justice of Pernambuco, Chief Justice Esterio Ramos Galvao, has also received death threats as a result of his efforts against corruption in the court system. According to Mr. Benvenuto de Lima, police have been unable to identify those who carried out the July 23 attack on him.

HELIO BICUDO THREATENED

On June 8, 1993, Hélio Bicudo, a well-known lawyer and Federal Senator from the state of São Paulo, confirmed having received death threats from the military police of São Paulo. According to the *Folha de Sao Paulo* newspaper of June 9, 1993, an unnamed policeman told Mr. Bicudo that three or four colonels in command of the São Paulo Military Police had discussed how to eliminate the Senator in a manner that would appear to be an accident. The paper went on to report that the death threats were motivated by two legal reform efforts in which Mr. Bicudo is involved. One would grant jurisdiction over crimes committed by the military police to the civilian judicial system rather than the military courts. The second is a proposal to demilitarize the military police by an amendment to the Brazilian Constitution.

MARCIA MARIA EUGENIO DE CARVALHO — KILLED

Lawyer Marcia Maria Eugenio de Carvalho and a client, Odete Cavalcante Medeiros, were assassinated on January 29, 1993 while driving in Ms. Carvalho's car on the highway near Bonito, in the state of Pernambuco. Three hired gunmen in a car belonging to a local sugarcane mill owner ambushed Ms. Carvalho's car and killed her and Ms. Medeiros with a 12-gauge shotgun. Justice official John Kennedy de Menezes Melo, a passenger in the car, escaped death by hiding in the back seat. Police investigators concluded that the crime was a planned assassination, intended only to kill Ms. Carvalho. When the gunmen realized they had mistakenly shot Ms. Medeiros, they gave chase and opened fire again on Ms. Carvalho.

According to the *Diário de Pernambuco* newspaper of April 2, 1993, the mill owner, Verinaldo José de Oliveira, is believed to have sought revenge against Ms. Carvalho for sponsoring a case against him for violating the rights of his workers. Furthermore, the Pastoral Land Commission learned that workers in the area had received death threats if they dared to bring any legal proceedings against Mr. Oliveira.

According to the Centro Luiz Freire, a human rights organization in Pernambuco, special police investigator Dr. Fausto Martins identified Verinaldo José de Oliveira, Edilson Martins da Silva and Jose Luiz Carlos as the authors of Ms. Carvalho's homicide. Testimonies by five eyewitnesses helped identify da Silva and Carlos as the gunmen. According to the *Diário de Pernambuco* of April 1, 1993, Carlos was found dead shortly after the killing; his death was seen by investigators as a way of protecting the intellectual author of the crime. On March 31, 1993, Verinaldo de Oliveira was accused with intellectual authorship of the murder. He has denied any involvement. The case remains with a representative of the Judicial Public Ministry of the town of Bonito and no further legal action has been taken.

SISTER CECILIA PETRINA DE CARVALHO ATTACKED, THREATENED

Sister Cecilia Petrina de Carvalho, a nun and lawyer for the Pastoral Land Commission in the state of Bahia, was shot and wounded on October 22, 1993. According to a report by the Pastoral Land Commission, Sister Cecilia had been receiving death threats from landowners in connection with her representation of peasants involved in land disputes in the region. On October 22, as she was driving from the town of Itiuba to the village of Cacimbas in Bahia State, accompanied by town councillor Analdino Laranjeira, a hooded gunman opened fire on Sister Cecilia's car, wounding her in the leg. The Secretary of Public Security has designated the regional police chief of Senhor Bonfim to investigate the incident. However, according to a report by Amnesty International, lawyers acting for Sister Cecilia have expressed concern at police delays in conducting an inspection of the scene of the crime and in carrying out ballistic tests.

Sister Cecilia has worked as a lawyer for the Pastoral Land Commission for more than eight years. She has represented peasants in legal disputes with landowners and land claimants. Before the October 22 shooting, Sister Cecilia and Father Luis Tonetto, a priest and local labor unionist, had received death threats related to a dispute between workers and owners of the Jabuticaba ranch in the municipality of Andorinha. In that case, although the peasants had gained a preliminary ruling in their favor for the demarcation of communal lands, the land claimant in dispute with them had allegedly continued to destroy vegetation and intimidate peasants.

ALVARO RIBEIRO COSTA
DOMINGOS DUTRA THREATENED

On May 14, 1993, in the town of Buriti in the northeastern state of Maranhão, Assistant Attorney General Alvaro Ribeiro Costa, human rights lawyer and state representative Domingos Dutra and several other human rights advocates were prevented by police officials from investigating charges of violence against residents of the Belém settlement. According to the Pastoral Land Commission, six military police ignored the presence of a federal authority, and intimidated the visiting lawyers and advocates while the settlement was destroyed by bulldozers. When Assistant Attorney General Costa demanded to see the commanding officer's identification and his written orders to evacuate the settlement, the commander refused and said only that he was following orders from higher authority. The settlement was destroyed by bulldozers belonging to the Grupo João Santos, a large landowner in the area and Brazil's second largest manufacturer of cement. The Grupo João Santos claims that it owns the Belem settlement; settlers who have lived there for fifty years dispute the claim.

The May 14 incident was not the first violent eviction at Belém. On March 16, 1993, 18 heavily armed military police under the command of Járcio de Souza, together with several gunmen contracted by the Grupo João Santos, invaded the property and forced settlers to leave, threatening to kill any who stayed. They also apprehended four Belém farmworkers and took them to a factory belonging to the company, where they allegedly tortured the four men, forced them to eat cow feed and to wear metal collars used for farm animals, doused them in gasoline and threatened to burn them alive. The workers were finally brought to the Buriti police station after the intervention of human rights lawyer Domingos Dutra. After their release, an independent commission was formed to investigate the events at Belem, made up of Mr. Dutra and representatives of the Brazilian Charity Organization of Maranhão, the Pastoral Council of Fishermen, the Pastoral Land Commission of Maranhão, the Maranhão Society for the Defense of Human Rights, Bishop Walter Carrijo of the local Diocese of Brejo, and state representatives Luiz Vila Nova and Benedito Coroba.

On May 17, 1993, after the intimidation of Mr. Dutra, Mr. Costa and their colleagues, Brazilian Attorney General Aristides Junqueira requested the Federal Police to open an inquiry into the violent events at Belém. In protest at this investigation, District Judge Edine Couto Bacelar denied that there had been any harassment or intimidation of Mr. Costa, Mr. Dutra or their colleagues on May 14. Although Judge Bacelar denied ordering the evacuation of the Belém settlement, she later admitted that she had declared the Grupo João Santos to be the rightful owners of the land. According to the Pastoral Land Commission, Judge Bacelar had also issued two court orders against the settlers without ever visiting the settlement. She claimed that the military police and gunmen at the site were necessary to protect employees of the Grupo João Santos, and that the company had tried unsuccessfully to negotiate with the settlers.

On May 19, 1993, the General Magistrate of the Public Ministry, Gervásio da Silva Ribeiro Filho, announced an inquiry into the conduct of District Judge Bacelar because of Mr. Costa's assertion that she had deliberately concealed the violent practices of the military police against the Belém settlers. According to lawyer José do Carmo of the Pastoral Land Commision, the case is moving slowly in the high courts.

LAURO RIBEIRO ESCOBAR JUNIOR
STELLA KUHLMAN
MARCO ANTONIO FERREIRA LIMA
PAULO MARAFANTI
ANTONIO AUGUSTO NEVES THREATENED, HARASSED

According to the newspaper *Folha de São Paulo* of October 22 and December 17, 1993, judges Lauro Ribeiro Escobar Junior, Paulo Marafanti and Antonio Augusto Neves, and prosecutors Stella Kuhlman and Marco Antonio Ferreira Lima of the Military Justice Department of the state of São Paulo received death threats over a nine-month period in 1993. The threats were delivered to their homes as well as to the offices of the State Council for the Defense of Human Rights.

The threats appear to stem from the involvement of these judges and prosecutors in a number of controversial cases involving the military police. In addition to the civilian police, Brazil has a military police division that was instituted during the military regime of 1964-1985. In the 1970s the state of Sao Paulo created a special section of the military police, known as ROTA (*Rondas Ostensivas Tobias de Aguiar*), to combat guerrillas and bank robbers; other states quickly followed Sao Paulo's example. ROTA officers were encouraged to kill "bandits" and in many cases were given raises or extra vacations according to the number they killed. Today some states have dismantled the ROTA division; it still exists, however, in São Paulo. ROTA has proved notoriously difficult to reform, in part because many of those promoted to senior positions within it are individuals involved in human rights abuses during the period of military rule.

In July 1993, Prosecutor Marco Antonio Ferreira Lima accused five ROTA agents of forming a kidnapping ring that targeted wealthy businessmen. Four of the five policemen were sentenced to prison terms of 14-20 years. Mr. Lima discovered a bomb planted in his car on October 21, 1993, soon after receiving a threatening telephone call warning him that he would die in a car explosion. In a deposition given on November 19, 1993, prosecutor Stella Kuhlman stated that she began receiving death threats after she tried and convicted police officer Daniel Viana of the ROTA 148 division for kidnapping, robbery and two murders. She was also followed by an unmarked car driven by two ROTA officers. Judge Lauro Escobar received a letter containing a bullet hole and a picture of a machine gun with the message, "You will be next."

The five judges and prosecutors believe that the death threats against them are intended to prevent their continued investigations and prosecutions of ROTA members involved in extra-judicial assaults, assassinations and kidnappings. They have sent a report to the Ministry of Justice, accusing São Paulo governor Luiz Antonio Fleury Filho, State Attorney General Araldo Dal Pozzo and the Commander of the Military Police of knowing about the death threats but declining to take any action to deter them.

PAULO COELHO PEREIRA KILLED

Lawyer Paulo Coelho Pereira was shot to death in the doorway of his home in Boa Vista on February 19, 1993, the night he was elected to serve as federal counselor for the Brazilian Bar Association (OAB) in the northern state of Roraima. According to the Bar Association, Mr. Pereira had received several death threats in 1992 after denouncing corruption among Roraima state officials, including members of the judiciary. His name also appeared on a death list of nine people, including five other lawyers, that circulated in Boa Vista (see above). Before his murder, Mr. Pereira had been the object of so-called "white punishment," by which he was effectively prevented by the court system from processing his cases. His election as federal counselor for the Bar Association would have given him more power to reform the Tribunal Court system.

Police investigators traced the car used by the gunmen to the Tribunal Court of Roraima. In addition, Mr. Pereira left a tape recording describing his investigation into corruption in the state Tribunal Court system. Mr. Pereira's investigative efforts, conducted jointly with his fellow lawyer, Marivaldo Freire, have resulted in the voiding of last year's Tribunal elections and questioned the legality of the Governor's appointment of Tribunal Chief Justice Luiz Gonzaga Batista and Justice Elair Francisco.

On March 23, 1993, two former police officers, Carlos Antonio Sales de Santana and Marcos Andre Cavalcante, were jailed. The men had been positively identified by Mr. Pereira's sons as two of the killers. Before going to work for the state of Roraima, both men had been expelled from the military police force of the state of Alagoas after allegations of their involvement in an earlier murder. According to the *Jornal do Brasil* newspaper of May 4, 1993, Luiz Gonzaga Batista Junior, son of the Roraima Chief Justice, was indicted as the author of the murder of Paulo Coelho Pereira and arrested by Federal Police in his home state of Ceara after more than a month on the run. At the time of Mr. Pereira's death, Mr. Batista Junior was chief detective of the Center of Operations of the Roraima civil police. His brother, Luiz Antonio, also remains a suspect in the case. Chief Justice Luiz Gonzaga Batista has been forced to retire as head of the Tribunal Court of Roraima.

COLOMBIA

RAFAEL BARRIOS MENDIVIL THREATENED, FLED COUNTRY

LAWYER-TO-LAWYER NETWORK APPEAL, DECEMBER 1993

Dr. Rafael Barrios Mendivil fled Colombia on October 9, 1993 after receiving repeated death threats. Dr. Barrios Mendivil, a noted human rights lawyer, was the president of the *Corporación Colectivo de Abogados "José Alvear Restrepo"* in the Colombian capital, Bogotá. The threats on his life came in response to his involvement in prosecuting three high-profile cases of extra-judicial killings allegedly committed by members of the Colombian security forces. In addition to receiving telephone calls warning him that he would be killed unless he dropped his work on these three sensitive cases, Dr. Barrios Mendivil had been under surveillance by agents of the security forces.

Dr. Barrios Mendivil had filed charges in an administrative tribunal against members of the Colombian security forces for the alleged detention, torture and assassination of university student Alvaro Moreno Moreno in 1991. In November 1993, the tribunal found that Moreno had been captured and killed by members of SIJIN (an intelligence arm of the National Police), and that evidence of the crime had been concealed and later covered up by the National Police. The tribunal awarded reparations to members of Moreno's family. The Colombian State Council, the court of last resort in cases against state agents, is considering an appeal. Meanwhile, the Office of the Attorney General has allowed the police agents implicated in the crime to go free.

In a separate case, Dr. Barrios Mendivil had brought charges against members of the National Police for the massacre on December 16, 1991 of at least 20 Paez Indians who had been occupying a ranch known as El Nilo in the province of Cauca. A report issued by the General Prosecutor in October 1992 affirmed that strong evidence pointed to the police officials being responsible for the massacre. Nonetheless, on July 21, 1993, the Human Rights Prosecutor-Delegate exonerated the officials charged. In August 1993, the Human Rights Ombudsman requested that the case be reconsidered, and the decision to continue with the prosecution passed to the General Prosecutor. The attorneys prosecuting the case prior to Dr. Barrios Mendivil--Dr. Carlos Edgar Torres and Dr. Rodolfo Alvarez--were murdered in January 1992, with clear evidence that their killing was in reprisal for their work on the El Nilo case. (These cases are described in the 1992 edition of *In Defense of Rights.*) Dr. Oscar Elías López, a lawyer acting on behalf of the Regional Indigenous Council of Cauca (*Consejo Regional Indígena del Cauca,* or CRIC), was also killed in May 1992, reportedly for his work on the case.

The third case that prompted threats against Dr. Barrios Mendivil was the massacre on April 7, 1991 of 17 people on a public bus in Los Uvos, in the province of Cauca. In April 1993 the General Prosecutor brought charges against members of the Colombian army and requested further investigation of an army general, a colonel, three majors and a lieutenant suspected of covering up the crime. The General Prosecutor also found irregularities in the investigation carried out by the military court and recommended disciplinary proceedings against those members of the military responsible for the cover-up.

Since Dr. Barrios Mendivil left Colombia, the cases of Alvaro Moreno Moreno, El Nilo and Los Uvos have been taken over by his colleagues at the *Corporación Colectivo de Abogados.*

CARLOS ALBERTO CAICEDO MENDEZ — KILLED

Laywer Carlos Alberto Caicedo Méndez was ambushed and murdered by six men on October 8, 1993 in the township of La Palma, in the department of Cundinamarca. His killers identified themselves as members of the 22nd Front of the Revolutionary Armed Forces of Colombia (*Fuerzas Armadas Revolucionarias de Colombia,* or FARC), a guerrilla organization.

EDGARDO CONTRERAS LEAL KILLED

Dr. Edgardo Contreras Leal, an investigating lawyer with the Technical Corps of the Public Order Prosecutor's Office in Cucutá, in the department of Norte de Santander, was assassinated on April 27, 1993, along with his colleague Carlos Eduardo Hernández Ordoñez. The two men were in the process of issuing a summons in the Galán neighborhood of the city of Barrancabermeja. Galán is known as a high-risk neighborhood, or "red zone," and judicial officials generally refuse to deal with gathering evidence or conducting other proceedings there. According to the Andean Commission of Jurists (Colombian section), Dr. Contreras and Mr. Hernández are believed to have been assassinated by members of a local civilian militia.

GERARDO DAZA GARCIA KILLED

Laywer and human rights activist Dr. Gerardo Daza García was found dead in his office in the city of Tunja, department of Boyacá, on April 5, 1993. He appeared at first to have hanged himself. However, an autopsy concluded that he had been murdered. The Andean Commission of Jurists (Colombian Section), as well as local press reports, have indicated that his murder was motivated by his human rights advocacy, although no particular group or individual has been identified as the assassin.

NANCY FIALLO ARAQUE THREATENED

Dr. Nancy Fiallo Araque is the director of the Foundation for the Promotion of Popular Culture and Education (*Fundación para la Promoción de la Cultura y la Educación Popular*, or FUNPROCEP). Dr. Fiallo received constant threats against her life throughout 1993, which were prompted by her legal work in defense of human rights in Bucaramanga, in the Magdalena Medio, one of the most violence-ridden regions of the country.

HUMBERTO GEOVO ALMANZA HARASSED, THREATENED

Lawyer Humberto Geovo Almanza is the ombudsman (*personero*) of the town of San Vicente de Chucurí in the department of Santander. Under the 1991 Colombian Constitution, the municipal *personero* is responsible for human rights monitoring. This role has pitted Dr. Geovo against certain members of the military, which is engaged in armed confrontations with the guerrillas and suspected guerrilla collaborators. He was the victim of a pattern of serious harassment and death threats by paramilitary forces under the command of the Colombian army, and fled San Vicente de Chucurí, fearing for his safety, in early 1993. He has sought guarantees of protection from the armed forces in order to return to carry out his work without fear for his life, but these have been denied. A further request for protection has been made through the Prosecutor-Delegate for the Armed Forces (the Public Ministry official responsible for overseeing the military's compliance with Colombian laws), but to date there has been no response.

FABIO HERNENDEZ FERERO
ANTONIO SUAREZ NINO DISCIPLINARY ACTION

Disciplinary sanctions were imposed on State Prosecutor Fabio Hernéndez and criminal investigations judge Antonio Suárez Niño as a result of their work on behalf of fellow judges and lawyers. Mr. Hernéndez and Judge Suárez are vice-president and acting president, respectively, of ASONAL JUDICIAL, the organization that represents lawyers and judges employed by the Colombian judicial system. On November 19, 1992, members of ASONAL JUDICIAL organized a day of national protest. The Attorney General brought criminal charges against those involved, and Mr. Hernández and Mr. Suárez represented the defendants. On June 18, 1993, the Attorney General imposed unspecified disciplinary sanctions against the two lawyers.

DR. EDUARDO LANCHEROS ABRIU KILLED

Dr. Eduardo Lancheros Abriú, an investigating lawyer with the Technical Corps of the Prosecutor General's Office of the Department of Antioquia, was assassinated in Medellín on March 12, 1993 by an unidentified woman. The Andean Commission of Jurists (Colombian section) believes that Dr. Lancheros' death was intended to deter the investigations that he had been conducting into a number of killings in the Medellín region. In the months preceding his assassination, a wave of violence in the region had claimed the lives of labor union officials and leaders of two political parties, the Patriotic Union (*Unión Patriótica*) and the Movement for Hope, Peace and Liberty (*Movimiento Esperanza, Paz y Libertad*).

FREDDY YESID MARTINEZ MURILLO
JAIME BENITO PARRADO KILLED

Lawyers Jaime Benito Parrado and Freddy Yesid Martínez Murillo, investigators with the Technical Corps of the Prosecutor General's Office, were abducted on February 4, 1993 by a group of armed men near the city of Turbo in the Urabá region of northwestern

Colombia. Their bodies were found four days later, with signs of torture and multiple bullet wounds. Their abductors were reportedly members of a dissident faction of the People's Liberation Army (*Ejército Popular de Liberación*, or EPL), a guerrilla organization. According to the Colombian Section of the Andean Commission of Jurists, the likely motive for the killings was that Mr. Martínez and Mr. Parrado had been involved in the investigation of the kidnapping and disappearance of two Europeans, a Finn and a Swede, at the hands of EPL dissidents.

ALVARO MENESES
ANONYMOUS LAWYER THREATENED

Alvaro Meneses is the director of the legal department of the Colombian Petroleum Corporation (*Empresa Colombiana de Petróleo*, or ECOPETROL). Together with another unnamed ECOPETROL lawyer, he received an anonymous threat on May 20, 1993, written in the form of an invitation to their funeral. As a likely motive, the Colombian Section of the Andean Commission of Jurists has pointed to the role of the two lawyers as legal advisers on a bill that would establish public ownership of petrolem deposits in the region of Cusiana, in the department of Casanare. The proposed law has been controversial among private claimants to the subsoil in question, and the author of the bill, Senator Eduardo Chávez López, has also received death threats. A conservative press commentary published on May 28 condemned the proposed bill as a triumph of the "parliamentary guerrilla movement."

JESUS ANTONIO MONTOYA OSPINA KILLED

Human rights lawyer Dr. Jesús Antonio Montoya Ospina was murdered in Cali on December 14, 1993 by two unidentified assassins. Dr. Montoya, a founding member of the Bogotá-based Committee of Solidarity with Political Prisoners (*Comité de Solidaridad con los Presos Políticos*), worked as a defense attorney for trade unionists and political prisoners and was an active member of the leftist Patriotic Union party. At the time of his death, Dr. Montoya was representing a group of trade union members claiming compensation from the state for their arbitrary arrest, torture and imprisonment by the Army's Third Brigade in Cali in 1990. Another of the union members' attorneys, Alirio Pedraza Becerra, had been "disappeared" in July 1990.

According to witnesses, Dr. Montoya arrived at a meeting with a local housing committee in the Belalcazar neighborhood of Cali on December 14. He found the building in which the meeting was to take place closed and two gunmen waiting for him in the doorway. An argument ensued during which Dr. Montoya was injured. He attempted to flee, but was pursued by the gunmen and shot 14 times in the chest, killing him instantly. The killers escaped with Dr. Montoya's briefcase of documents.

HECTOR TORRES THREATENED

Dr. Hector Torres, Municipal Counsellor of the town of La Uribe, in the province of Meta, has received anonymous death threats, allegedly issued by members of the First Mobile Brigade of the Colombian Army, which has heavily militarized the area surrounding La Uribe. The Meta region has been the scene of escalating conflict between the opposition Revolutionary Armed Forces of Colombia (*Fuerzas Armadas Revolucionarias de Colombia*, or FARC) and government forces. Human rights advocacy is viewed with suspicion by the military, which generally suspects advocates of sympathizing, if not actively collaborating, with the guerrillas.

On February 26, 1993, Dr. Torres accompanied a delegation from an international human rights organization on a fact-finding mission in La Uribe. The delegation conducted a number of interviews with local citizens the following day, and Dr. Torres himself was also interviewed. The following morning, Dr. Torres and three other individuals who had been interviewed discovered that anonymous written death threats had been pushed under their doors during the night. The threats were reported to local authorities, but no investigation has been undertaken to date.

EDUARDO UMANA MENDOZA THREATENED

LAWYER-TO-LAWYER NETWORK APPEAL, MAY 1993

Bogotá human rights lawyer Dr. Eduardo Umaña Mendoza received constant anonymous death threats throughout 1993. As reported in last year's edition of *In Defense of Rights*, Dr. Umaña received similar telephone calls in 1991 and 1992, threatening to kill him if he did not cease his human rights defense work. These threats appear to stem in part from Dr. Umaña's work on the TELCOM case, in which sixteen telecommunications technicians were charged with committing terrorist acts. The technicians were accused of sabotaging computer equipment belonging to the state-owned telephone and telecommunications company TELCOM, in protest against the government's plans to privatize the company. The workers had intended to go on strike to protest the planned privatization, but the government declared the strike illegal and police authorities broke up the union meeting at which strike plans were being discussed. It is alleged that the sixteen workers then resorted to sabotage of the company's computer system. The Colombian telephone service was shut down for seven days as a result.

The sixteen technicians were initially charged under anti-terrorist legislation decreed by President César Gaviria during a state of emergency in 1988 and converted into permanent legislation in November 1991. The charges carried penalties of up to 60 years' imprisonment. After much national and international protest, the case was transferred from the Public Order jurisdiction, specially designed to try cases of alleged terrorism and drug trafficking, to the ordinary courts and the detainees were released from prison pending trial. Colombian rights advocates, including Dr. Umaña, have expressed grave concern over the past two years that anti-terrorist legislation is being used to quash legitimate social and labor protest.

Dr. Eduardo Umaña is also currently defending Francisco Galán, the EPL guerrilla leader arrested in December 1992 on charges of terrorism. The threats against Dr. Umaña are also presumed to relate to his work on this case.

RICARDO VILLA SALCEDO KILLED

Ricardo Villa Salcedo, a practicing lawyer and former senator who remained politically active, was assassinated on January 8, 1993. The lawyer had accused the mayor of Santa Marta of receiving personal benefits that were connected to money from a group of extortionists. He had previously denounced the mayor for electoral fraud, precipitating his resignation. Mr. Villa Salcedo was shot seven times. (This case was reported in the 1992 edition of *In Defense of Rights*; the date of Mr. Villa Salcedo's death was erroneously given there as December 23, 1992.)

ANONYMOUS CONSTITUTIONAL COURT MAGISTRATE THREATENED

A magistrate of the Constitutional Court received a death threat by telephone on August 23, 1993, demanding the reversal of a decision issued by the Council of State that had declared null and void the election of the mayor of the city of Santa Marta, the capital of the department of Magdalena. The Constitutional Court ultimately ruled in favor of the decision of the Council of State.

ANONYMOUS CONSTITUTIONAL COURT MAGISTRATE THREATENED

On September 10, 1993, an anonymous death threat was delivered to another Constitutional Court magistrate who had delivered an opinion reviewing the unconstitutionality of a law adopting a Public Order decree as permanent legislation. The legislation under review was Law 15 of 1992, which adopted as permanent legislation Articles 1, 3 and 4 of the Internal Commotion Decree, regulating the crimes that would fall within the competence of Public Order judges and magistrates, as well as restrictions on the habeas corpus rights of detainees charged with narcotics trafficking and terrorism. Later, the Office of the Secretary of the Constitutional Court received a telephone call threatening that the magistrates would pay with their lives if they "let free the detained narco-traffickers and terrorists." The source of the threat is unknown. The Constitutional Court handed down its opinion on Law 15 on October 2, 1993; a majority declared Article 1 of the law constitutional, but Article 3 unconstitutional.

COMITE REGIONAL PARA LA DEFENSA DE LOS DERECHOS HUMANOS (CREDHOS)

THREATENED

Since May 1993, members of CREDHOS, a human rights organization in the conflict-torn region of Magdalena Medio, have been the victims of threats and harassment by officials of the Army's Nueva Granada battalion in the city of Barrancabermeja. CREDHOS has openly denounced human rights abuses committed by guerrilla organizations in the region, as well as by the armed forces and paramilitary groups operating under the command of, or with the support of, the military.

On May 27, 1993, CREDHOS issued a press release denouncing human rights violations by the Nueva Granada Battalion against the civilian population of Barrancabermeja. At the request of CREDHOS, the Regional Prosecutor and the Municipal Ombudsman undertook an investigation on June 29 into information concerning the detention and torture of three civilians at the base. These actions appear to have triggered the harassment of CREDHOS's president by senior officers of the battalion, who have accused him of working on behalf of the guerrillas.

Similar accusations in the past have been followed by physical attacks against CREDHOS workers. In 1992, three members of CREDHOS were killed in circumstances suggesting extra-judicial execution. Other members have been the target of death threats and harassment, including intensive surveillance by state security agents. Although the Colombian government has condemned the attacks on CREDHOS and has promised full investigations into the incidents that took place in 1992 and 1993, those responsible have not been identified or prosecuted.

MEDELLIN JUDGES AND MAGISTRATES ATTACKED

On January 7, 1993, a car-bomb exploded in a housing unit in Medellín, in an apparent assassination attempt against several judges and magistrates who live in the building. Two unidentified persons abandoned a vehicle containing 100 kilograms of dynamite in the basement of the building. The explosion killed the two suspects, and caused a fire which injured 20 people. Another car-bomb of similar size had exploded in the same neighborhood a month earlier.

OTHER COLOMBIAN LEGAL PROFESSIONALS KILLED

The widespread and indiscriminate violence in Colombia presents unusual problems of documentation in ascribing responsibility for human rights violations. In each of the eight killings described above, there is a strong presumption either of the involvement of state agents, or of the murder being precipitated by the victim's human rights advocacy or involvement in politically sensitive cases. These eight deaths, however, give only a small hint of the climate of pervasive violence in which Colombian lawyers and judges must operate. In most of the country, there are at least four competing sources of armed authority — overnment security forces, organized paramilitary groups, leftist guerrilla organizations and drug traffickers. With violence rampant, and central government authority often feeble, most murders go unsolved after only a perfunctory investigation.

According to a recent report of the Colombian Section of the Andean Commission of Jurists,[1] at least 30 legal professionals were murdered in 1993, in addition to the eight cases listed by name above. Four of the 30 were investigating lawyers attached to regional prosecutors' offices; the remaining 26 were practicing lawyers. Five of the dead were representing drug traffickers, and responsibility for their deaths was claimed by an organization calling itself Persecuted by Pablo Escobar (*Perseguidos por Pablo Escobar*, or PEPES); one was killed by guerrillas; one was shot dead when he refused to obey an order to stop by a Colombian soldier posted outside the US Embassy in Bogota; one death was the result of a common criminal assault. In the remaining 22 cases, both the identity of the killers and their motive remain a mystery.

CUBA

LUIS ALBERTO PITA SANTOS — IMPRISONED

Luís Alberto Pita Santos, a former law professor and president and founder of the Association of Defenders of Political Rights, has been imprisoned since October 1991 for taking part in a press

[1]"Violencia contra Jueces y Abogados en Colombia 1993," informe preparado por Guido Alberto Bonilla Pardo, Bogotá, January 1994.

conference organized by several dissident groups. In March 1992, he was tried and convicted of "contempt" for offending the head of State, as well as of "clandestine printing" and illegal association. After spending seven months in pre-trial solitary confinement, Mr. Pita Santos was sentenced to five years in prison. According to sources contacted by Human Rights Watch/Americas, Mr. Pita Santos is presently confined in Camagüey Prison, where he is reportedly chained at the ankle during daytime hours as punishment for protesting his continued incarceration. He has also reportedly been beaten.

DOMINICAN REPUBLIC

JUDGE SOMNIA VARGAS TEJADA — DISCIPLINARY ACTION

LAWYER-TO-LAWYER
NETWORK APPEAL, JANUARY 1994

On September 22, 1993, the Dominican Supreme Court ordered Judge Somnia Vargas Tejada, one of five members of the Court of Appeal of Santo Domingo, to be transferred to the town of San Juan de la Maguana, some 275 kilometers from the capital, close to the Haitian border. Judge Vargas was given no reason for the transfer order, and refused to comply, claiming that the order was unconstitutional and that it was motivated by critical remarks she had made in the Dominican media and other public fora about defects in the country's penal and judicial systems. Judge Vargas, a member of the Court of Appeal since 1987, was for many years legal adviser to the non-governmental Union for the Defense of Human Rights. She is also a professor of journalism at the Autonomous University of Santo Domingo.

In the weeks preceding the Supreme Court's order, Judge Vargas had criticized a number of alleged abuses by police and judicial authorities. On July 14, 1993, she expressed concern about frequent reports of physical coercion by police to extract confessions. Judge Vargas also drew attention to the suborning of judges and police investigators by drug cartels, which have made increasing use of the Dominican Republic in recent years as a transit point for narcotics shipments to the United States. At a September 5, 1993 seminar on human rights in the Dominican Republic, Judge Vargas criticized the appointment process for new Dominican judges, arguing that judges are frequently appointed for partisan political reasons. She urged that the government take measures to insure the independence of the judiciary.

On December 13, 1993, Judge Vargas lodged a protest with the Attorney General, citing irregularities in her transfer. Neither the Supreme Court nor the Attorney General has responded to her appeals.

EL SALVADOR

JOSE MARIA MENDEZ   THREATENED, FLED COUNTRY

In November 1993, attorney José María Méndez and his wife received the first in a series of anonymous death threats. He had recently been named "Lawyer of the Century" by three of El Salvador's bar associations, and had become a well-known figure as a result of his decision to remain in El Salvador throughout the war and continue his advocacy.

During the campaign leading up to El Salvador's first post-war elections in March 1994, many candidates and their supporters were the targets of renewed threats of violence. There was also an upsurge of death-squad killings of the sort that had characterized the war. According to Francisco Lima, a friend of Mr. Méndez's and a candidate for Vice-President for the Democratic Convergence party (*Convergencia Democrática*) in the March 1994 elections, "They told [Mr. Méndez] to convince me to withdraw from the campaign, and if he didn't succeed, they were going to harm his wife. They gave him until December 15." José María Méndez and his wife fled El Salvador on December 14.

RENE MEDECADEL PERLA JIMENEZ THREATENED

Dr. René Medecadel Perla Jiménez is a law professor at the National University of El Salvador and a member of a prominent, politically active family. His life was threatened twice in September 1993. On the first occasion, on September 14, Mr. Perla Jiménez received a telephone message from someone who claimed to be calling from the Salvadoran Lawyers Association. Mr. Perla Jiménez was told that he had three days to leave El Salvador; if he failed to do so, he would be killed for his alleged work in support of the Farabundo Martí Front for National Liberation (FMLN). Two days later, on September 16, he received a second anonymous threat by telephone, again citing his alleged work for the FMLN. This time the caller identified himself as a member of the *Maximiliano Hernández Martínez* death squad.

In addition to his teaching duties, Dr. Perla Jiménez is also the representative of the National University on the National Council on the Judiciary, which screens candidates for judgeships. The council was formed in 1989, but its membership criteria were changed pursuant to constitutional reforms introduced in 1991. Since then, the council has been more broadly representative of the full spectrum of Salvadoran society. As a result, however, its activities have become more politically contentious as the conservative-dominated Supreme Court has fought to maintain its political control over the Council. The report of the United Nations Truth Commission pointed to the Salvadoran judiciary as a contributing factor in the climate of impunity for acts of political violence, and implicated several members of the Supreme Court in miscarriages of justice in human rights cases. The Truth Commission also recommended a number of institutional changes in the judiciary, including the replacement of all sitting members of the Supreme Court, but these have been ignored by the present conservative government.

JOSE EDUARDO
PINEDA VALENZUELA KILLED

LAWYER-TO-LAWYER NETWORK
UPDATE, MARCH 1993

Lawyer José Eduardo Pineda Valenzuela died on March 17, 1993, as a result of injuries suffered in a shooting the previous year. As the 1992 edition of *In Defense of Rights* reported, Mr. Pineda was attacked by two unidentified gunmen on July 31, 1992. He was a longtime member of the Human Rights Department of the Salvadoran Attorney General's office, the *Fiscalía*, and eventually became its director. In that capacity, he acted as lead prosecutor in the investigation of the 1989 murder of six Jesuit priests. He also served on the team that prosecuted two FMLN combatants for the 1991 murder of two US helicopter pilots. Mr. Pineda had been appointed to head one of the divisions of the Human Rights Ombudsman's office shortly before he was shot in July 1992.

FRANCISCO ARTURO PLEITEZ LEMUS KILLED

First Criminal Court Judge Francisco Arturo Pleitez Lemus was stabbed to death in front of his home on September 3, 1993. The National Police at first arrested three members of a local gang for the murder. Judge Pleitez had previously imprisoned ten members of the gang and had expressed a fear of reprisals. The gang members were later released, however, due to a lack of evidence.

The Ministry of Justice later concluded that the murder of Judge Pleitez was not the result of a common crime, but rather was related to his role in the controversial case of Roldán Antonio Castillo, a lawyer who was later convicted for the attempted kidnap of the daughter of a prominent opposition politician. According to Dr. Pleitez's daughter, the judge had received a number of death threats in the weeks prior to his death, which the family believed were connected to the Castillo case. One written threat stated: *"Corrupt Judge Pleitez Lemus, we are watching you."* Members of Castillo's family had allegedly offered money to Judge Pleitez Lemus in an effort to have him acquit Castillo of the kidnapping charges. At the time of his murder, Judge Pleitez was no longer handling the Castillo case, which had been passed up to another judge. Lawyers working on the case have requested the Supreme Court to provide improved security for them, as has the judge who oversaw the conviction.

GUATEMALA

RODOLFO AZMITIA JIMENEZ — THREATENED

Rodolfo Azmitia Jiménez, a human rights lawyer and legal director of the Center for the Investigation, Study and Promotion of Human Rights (CIEPRODH), was one of 24 people threatened with death in a letter circulated on March 27, 1993 by a clandestine rightist group. Those listed were accused of being "spokespersons for, defenders of and sympathizers with subversion and its organizations." They were given 72 hours to leave the country; failing this, they would be considered legitimate military targets. At the time of this threat, Mr. Azmitia was providing legal assistance to inhabitants of La Isla community who had been threatened with eviction. A second, similar mass death threat was circulated in October 1993 (see below, case of Fernando López, Vinicio Mejía Dávila, Otto Peralta and Juan José Rodil Peralta).

MARIO CABRERA RAMAZZINI — THREATENED

Mario Cabrera Ramazzini, a Public Ministry lawyer in the department of Sololá, received several death threats by telephone on September 9, 1993. The unidentified callers told him to renounce his profession and leave Sololá; otherwise he would have only a few days left to live. According to local press reports, the threats may have been connected to Mr. Cabrera Ramazzini's investigation into the murder of a youth in the San Antonio district of Sololá.

GUATEMALAN JURISTS ASSOCIATION
CECILIA ALVAREZ PAZ
FERNANDO RENE
DE LEON SOLANO
OSWALDO ENRIQUEZ ATTACKED, THREATENED

On the morning of September 10, 1993, a package bomb exploded in the offices of the Guatemalan Jurists Association (*Asociación Guatemalteca de Juristas*, or AGJ). The bomb had been intended for delivery to Cecilia Alvarez Paz, a lawyer and notary with the association. The explosion caused serious damage to furniture and documents, but no one was physically harmed.

Other members of the AGJ were periodically harassed during 1993. Fernando René de León Solano, secretary of the Association's executive board, reported that in early July he was often followed by two men wearing military boots and with military style haircuts. On July 12 a trade unionist visited Mr. de León and told him that the day before he had been abducted for several hours. While he was being interrogated, his captors questioned him about several people, including Mr. de León, whom they linked to the armed opposition. On July 21 and 23, two separate employees of a funeral home visited the AGJ offices, responding to anonymous phone calls telling them that a service might be necessary for Fernando de León. Oswaldo Enríquez, a lawyer and director of the AGJ, received death threats both before and after the bombing of the association's offices.

MARIO RENE DIAZ LOPEZ
HECTOR HUGO PEREZ AGUILERA
ISNARDO ROCA MORAN
MARIO GUILLERMO RUIZ WONG
CARLOS VILLATORO SHUNIMANN THREATENED

Magistrates Díaz López, Pérez Aguilera and Ruíz Wong of the Fourth Court of Appeals in Guatemala City repeatedly received anonymous threatening phone calls as well as an anonymous letter on April 23, 1993. The letter told the magistrates that their days "are numbered," and that it was time for the authors of the letter to apply "our own law, that of the gun." The letter was sent a few days before the court issued a verdict convicting and sentencing several soldiers for the 1991 massacre of 11 people on the highway to Taxisco Santa Rosa--the so-called *traileros* case. The Fourth Court also held jurisdiction at the time over two 1990 murder cases involving military defendants, that of Guatemalan anthropologist Myrna Mack Chang, and of U.S. citizen Michael Devine. The Second and Third Sentencing Judges, Isnardo Roca Morán and Carlos Villatoro Shunimann, were also threatened by anonymous letter because of their involvement in these key cases. In response, the Supreme Court provided 24-hour protection for the magistrates and their families. Earlier, in August 1992, the judges of this Appeals Court (comprising Mr. Ruíz Wong, Mr. Pérez Aguilera, and Napoleón Gutiérrez Vargas), received written and verbal threats when the court reversed several sentences previously handed down by military tribunals.

CARMEN ELLGUTTER THREATENED

Carmen Ellgutter, the judge for the Tenth Court of Appeals in Guatemala City, was threatened on unspecified dates in 1993. As a trial judge she had convicted Noel Beteta Alvarez, a member of a Guatemalan military unit, for the murder of anthropogist Myrna Mack Chang, sentencing him to 25 years in prison. The threats from Beteta's supporters were published in the Guatemalan press.

RICARDO GAMEZ LOPEZ DETAINED

Ricardo Gámez López, a lawyer in the office of the Human Rights Ombudsman in Huehuetenango in northwestern Guatemala, was kidnapped and detained by members of a Civil Defense Patrol (*patrulla de autodefensa civil*) on August 4, 1993. The patrols were created after a massive counterinsurgency campaign in 1982 and involve several hundred thousand men nationwide. Although military rule ended in 1985, the patrols have survived under three civilian presidencies. Their continued existence has been a matter of concern to Guatemalan and international human rights groups.

JOSE MARIA GIRON VILLATORO HARASSED

José Mariano Girón Villatoro, a staff member in the legal office of Covenant House (*Casa Alianza*) in Latin America, was stopped on January 18, 1993 by an unidentified man and asked about Bruce Harris, the Covenant House director. Harris is currently living in Mexico as the result of numerous death threats against him in Guatemala. The unidentified man and an associate then followed Mr. Girón's bus to the National Police Headquarters, where Mr. Girón got off and entered the building. The two men waited outside while Mr. Girón called another member of Covenant House. Mr. Girón escaped by leaving through a side entrance. The legal office of *Casa Alianza* has a history of advocacy involving the rights of Guatemalan street children, and often legally represents children who have been beaten or abused by police officials.

EULALIO GONZALEZ AYMARA
JUAN JOSE RODAS MARTINEZ
JORGE ALEJANDRO RODAS VASQUEZ
JORGE SAENZ LARA ATTACKED

Eulalio González Aymará, a lawyer and Investigating Penal Judge in Jalapa, was shot and wounded by various unidentified armed men in Jalapa on April 2, 1993. He was taken to the Hermano Pedro hospital in critical condition after the attack. Relatives of Mr. González confirmed that he had been threatened in Guatemala City a week earlier by an unidentified man who approached him on the street and warned him not to return to Jalapa. According to Juan Rivera Clavería, secretary to Guatemalan Supreme Court President, Judge Juan José Rodil Peralta, three other magistrates of the same court had also received several death threats. These magistrates were Jorge Alejandro Rodas Vásquez, Jorge Sáenz Lara and Juan Jóse Rodas Martínez. All four court officials have been transferred to the Supreme Court building in Guatemala City for their protection.

ENRIQUE GONZALEZ
RODRIGUEZ ATTACKED, THREATENED

Lawyer Enrique González Rodríguez failed to return home on February 28, 1993. He was found on March 2 by his wife in the intensive care section of the San Juan de Dios hospital in Guatemala City, suffering from concussion and lacerations. Mr. González had been brought to the hospital early in the morning of February 28 by volunteer firemen after a serious automobile accident. According to Mr. González, his car had been run off the road. Witnesses said that his car was being pursued by two other vehicles when it crashed into a guard rail. Blood alcohol tests at the hospital were negative. Mr. González is the representative for the family of Michael Devine, a U.S. citizen living in Guatemala who was murdered by a military squad in June 1990. At the time of the accident, Mr. González was appealing the acquittal of several members of the military charged in the murder. Mr. González was due to have appeared at a March 5 hearing on the case before the Fourth Court of Appeals in Guatemala City. His wife reported that Mr. González had been receiving death threats at their home and at his office prior to this incident.

MARIO SALVADOR JIMENEZ BARILLAS
HECTOR RAUL ORELLANA ALARCON
MARIA EUGENIA VILLASENOR VELARDE HARASSED

On September 10, 1993, these three magistrates of the Third Court of Appeals in Guatemala City were the target of a formal complaint *(antejuicio)* that local human rights groups believe was designed to harass them after they had returned guilty verdicts in a controversial case involving the police, as well as to deter them from acting similarly in a second case. The Third Court of Appeals had found members of the Hunapú Task Force guilty for the April 1992 murder of student Julio Cuc Quim, and sentenced them to 30 years imprisonment. Rather than taking the case to appeal, the defense lawyer for the Hunapú agents chose to file an *antejuicio* against the presiding magistrates in the case. At the time, the Third Court of

Appeals was also handling a case involving police brutality against peasants involved in a land dispute in the village of Cajolá. The magistrates subsequently found the defendants guilty and imposed suspended sentences.

FERNANDO LOPEZ
MARCO VINICIO MEJIA DAVILA
OTTO PERALTA
JUAN JOSE RODIL PERALTA THREATENED

A second death list, similar to the March letter that included the name of lawyer Rodolfo Azmitia Jiménez (see above), was circulated on October 5, 1993. This leaflet announced that "the war has started against a group of communists, which is why we have ordered a summary trial for treason against the fatherland...the traitors to the fatherland must be executed." Again, those named were given 72 hours to leave the country or risk being considered legitimate military targets. As in the earlier case, the 22 individuals named included journalists, trade unionists, development workers, human rights activists and legal professionals.

The four lawyers threatened in the October death list were Fernando López, a law professor at the University of San Carlos; attorney Marco Vinicio Mejía Dávila, then director of the Human Rights Office of the Archdiocese of Guatemala; Otto Peralta, executive coordinator of the Center for Popular Action and Legal Defense (CEPADEL) (see below); and Supreme Court President Juan José Rodil Peralta. Judge Rodil Peralta was specifically accused of meeting in Madrid, Spain with Guatemalan guerrilla commanders Gaspar Ilom and Rolando Morán, as well as with Nicaraguan Sandinista leaders, in order to plan "the final attack on

Guatemala City." The threat against Rodil Peralta was not limited to his person but pertained to all "the workers in the justice system who are involved with the guerrillas." While the March death list was anonymous, the October leaflet was signed in the name of the "Roberto Lorenzana Anti-Communist Movement." Roberto Lorenzana is believed to have been the founder, in 1966, of the infamous White Hand *(Mano Blanca)*, a rightist death squad linked to the Army's intelligence service.

LUIS MAZARIEGOS DISMISSED

Luís Mazariegos, President of the Association of Judges and Magistrates and formerly an investigating judge in Guatemala City, was removed from his post on December 22, 1993 by order of the Supreme Court. Judge Mazariegos has claimed that his removal from the bench was punishment for his effort to purge the Supreme Court of corruption and political cronyism, which began after an unsuccessful attempt by former President Jorge Serrano Elías in May 1993 to suspend the judicial and legislative branches. In dismissing Judge Mazariegos, the Supreme Court charged him with making arbitrary and unprofessional rulings in a number of criminal cases. Judge Mazariegos has received extensive support from the judiciary as well as from the Guatemalan College of Lawyers and Notaries.

LUIS MONTEFAR FEAR OF HARASSMENT

Luis Montefar, Justice of the Peace in the municipality of Chajul, department of El Quiché, fears that his life is in danger after witnessing the exhumation of three bodies in San Gaspar Chajul on October 8, 1993. The corpses were later identified as those of three men who had been reportedly kidnapped by members of the Civil Defense Patrols in December 1989. Mr. Montefar ordered an immediate investigation to determine those responsible for the murders, and now fears retribution by the powerful Civil Defense Patrols in the area. Amnesty International has intervened on Mr. Montefar's behalf, citing a pattern of reprisals against other local residents and officials involved in controversial human rights issues in the Chajul area. In June 1993, residents of the village of Chel were reportedly taken from their homes and beaten for studying the Constitution, and in August a similar occurrence was reported when a group of citizens tried to form a human rights association.

POPULAR CENTER FOR LEGAL ACTION
AND DEFENSE (CEPADEL)
URIAS BAUTISTA OROSCO
ALFONSO CARRERA LUNA
RODOLFO ANIBAL GARCIA HERNANDEZ
GILBERT MONROY
OTTO PERALTA
CARLOS RODRIGUEZ
GUSTAVO VASQUEZ PERALTA ATTACKED, HARASSED, THREATENED

CEPADEL is a legal aid clinic working on behalf of Guatemala's poor and indigenous populations. It is jointly organized and run by the University Students Association and the Law Students Association of the University of San Carlos in Guatemala City. Throughout 1993, CEPADEL faced repeated threats, harassment and physical attack.

In May 1993, while investigating a land rights dispute in Cantón Chupol de Chichicastenango, in the northwestern department of El Quiché, CEPADEL associates Rodolfo Aníbal García Hernández and Gilbert Monroy were fired on in broad daylight by uniformed elements of the Guatemalan army. The two men were in the process of taking testimony and photographs to substantiate the community's claim to a certain plot of land when a contingent of about ten soldiers opened fire on them from a distance of approximately a hundred meters and then pursued them. Mr. García Hernández and Mr. Monroy managed to escape unharmed in a pick-up truck. CEPADEL has continued its work on behalf of the community of Cantón Chupol and others with similar concerns, but has not returned to Chupol. Complaints lodged with Guatemala's Attorney General for Human Rights have yielded no results.

During June and August 1993, agents of the Department of Criminal Investigations of the National Police repeatedly entered the offices of CEPADEL, making specific inquiries about student demonstrators who had been arrested as well as asking more general questions about the nature of CEPADEL's legal work. These visits are of great concern in view of the history of the legal clinic: in August and September 1989, during the most recent previous attempt to open such a clinic, eleven students who composed the Executive Council of the University Students Association were abducted and disappeared. The bodies of five of them were subsequently found on the campus grounds. The fate of the remaining six has never been discovered, and no one has ever been arrested for the murders.

CEPADEL has also received regular telephone threats from anonymous callers, usually threatening death if a named member of CEPADEL fails to leave the country by a certain date. Although such calls are usually made to the CEPADEL office, 28-year-old Otto Peralta, the executive coordinator of CEPADEL and the most frequent target of these threats, has also received threatening calls at his home. One of the most prominent members of CEPADEL, Mr. Peralta was the special invited guest of Rigoberta Menchú Tum at her acceptance of the Nobel Peace Prize in 1992. He has also played a visible role in negotiations between the Guatemalan government and the URNG guerrilla movement.

JUAN JOSE RODAS MARINES
JORGE ALEJANDRO RODAS VASQUEZ
JORGE SAENZ LARA THREATENED

Juan José Rodas Marines, Jorge Alejandro Rodas Vásquez and Jorge Sáenz Lara are judges at the Fifth Chamber of the Court of Appeals in Jalapa. The three received death threats in April 1993, which may be connected to their investigations in a trial related to drug trafficking.

MOISES ULFRAN DE LEON THREATENED

Moises Ulfrán de León, a prosecutor with the Public Ministry, received anonymous telephone death threats in February, 1993. At the time he was in charge of proceedings in several controversial cases, including one involving allegations of corruption at Roosevelt Public Hospital and another against legislator Miguel Angel Montpepeque.

ROBERT CASSAGNOL HARASSED

Robert Cassagnol, an assistant Justice of the Peace in Thiotte, in southeastern Haiti, was terrorized by a gang of soldiers and armed civilians on October 27, 1993. The mob forced Mr. Cassagnol to abandon his post, reportedly because he was a sympathizer of deposed president Jean-Bertrand Aristide. In this case, as in many other reports of human rights violations in Haiti since the 1991 military coup, details are scanty. This primarily reflects fear of reprisals against informants, especially since the withdrawal of international human rights observers from the joint United Nations-Organization of American States mission (MICIVIH) in October 1993.

JEAN-CLAUDE CLERZEAU ASSAULTED, DETAINED

On April 1, 1993, Jean-Claude Clerzeau, a Justice of the Peace in Bombardopolis in northern Haiti, was beaten, kicked and arrested by police and soldiers who also illegally searched his house without a warrant. Judge Clerzeau was also a member of the Peasant Association of Bombardopolis, described by local military officials as the "brains of the *Lavalas* power." *Lavalas* is the grassroots political coalition that supports elected President Aristide.

The arrest took place during a police sweep ordered by Brigade Sergeant Elius, the senior police official in Bombardopolis, and approximately a dozen military personnel. (The local police post is staffed by military personnel; separation of the police and the armed forces was one of the crucial issues on which Haitian Justice Minister Guy Malary was working at the time of his murder.) During the sweep, soldiers beat and arrested local residents perceived as Aristide supporters. The police action was aimed in part at those who had distributed photographs of Aristide during a celebration on March 27-28 of the sixth anniversary of the promulgation of the Haitian Constitution.

When Judge Clerzeau demanded to know the grounds for his arrest, he was accused of "not having enough respect" for Sgt. Elius. After his beating, Judge Clerzeau was taken to the police post and held there for two hours. Because of the lack of detention facilities in Bombardopolis, the judge was then bound, placed on the floor of a pick-up truck under the feet of soldiers, and driven for two hours to Môle St. Nicolas. On arrival there, Judge Clerzeau was put in a jail cell with a common criminal who administered another beating at the direction of an unidentified policeman. At 8:00 that evening, Judge Clerzeau was released after the personal intercession of François Excéus, the second-ranking executive officer of the area and a distant relative.

The commander of the Northwest department, Lt. Col. Léopold Clerjeune, later confirmed that Judge Clerzeau's arrest had been ordered by Capt. Charles Pierre Gérard, military commander of Môle St. Nicolas, whose jurisdiction includes Bombardopolis. He added that pro-Aristide literature had been found at Judge Clerzeau's house during a search, and that the judge was guilty under the Haitian Penal Code of "inciting violence" and promoting the distribution of subversive material.

Judge Clerzeau had been named as Justice of the Peace by the constitutional government, replacing Novius Nogame, an appointee of the Duvalier dictatorship who had retired after a 34-year tenure. After Judge Clerzeau's arrest, Mr. Nogame was reinstated. On April

4, after his release from detention, Judge Clerzeau was warned that Sgt. Elius and another soldier were coming to his house. Fearing for his safety, the judge fled and is now in hiding in Port-au-Prince.

GERARD DALVIUS ATTACKED

On July 17, 1993, lawyer Gérard Dalvius, the second-ranking official (Secretary of State) in the Justice Ministry of the democratically elected government, was attacked by a group of armed men as he was about to enter his home. Mr. Dalvius's aggressors made threats against him and President Aristide after the attack. Mr. Dalvius has expressed the belief that state agents were responsible for the assault. The 1992 edition of *In Defense of Rights* reported earlier acts of violence against Mr. Dalvius by the then Port-au-Prince prosecutor, Lionel Dominique, who was later removed from his post.

CHARLES LUC KERLIN ATTACKED

Charles Luc Kerlin, a Justice of the Peace in the central town of Saut d'Eau, went to Port-au-Prince on December 8, 1993 to apply for political asylum in the United States. He reported that four soldiers had come to his house and beaten him because of his perceived sympathy for President Aristide.

GUY MALARY KILLED

LAWYER-TO-LAWYER NETWORK APPEAL,
OCTOBER 1993

On October 14, 1993, gunmen shot and killed Haitian lawyer and Minister of Justice Guy Malary, his driver and two of his bodyguards as they left the Justice Ministry in Port-au-Prince. According to bystanders, armed police and civilians chased away witnesses immediately after the murder and threatened to shoot news photographers at the scene. Mr. Malary, 50, was killed on the eve of the scheduled October 15 resignation of Gen. Raoul Cédras, the leader of Haiti's de facto military government, as called for in the U.N.-brokered Governor's Island Accord. His death came three days after US and Canadian troops were prevented from docking in Port-au-Prince harbor by a mob of armed civilians allowed into the port area by uniformed police.

Mr. Malary was appointed Minister of Justice by President Aristide in July 1993. Despite repeated threats on his life by police auxiliaries (*attachés*), Mr. Malary was one of the first Aristide-appointed cabinet members to occupy his office. As Justice Minister, he worked closely with human rights monitors from MICIVIH. On October 5, Mr. Malary presented the Haitian parliament with President Aristide's plan to form a new police force under the control of the Justice Ministry. As head of the ministry, Mr. Malary would have overseen efforts to retrain the police and would have been responsible for naming its new chief. Shortly before his killing, Mr. Malary was attempting to negotiate the retirement of Haitian Supreme Court President Emile Jonaissant, an ally of the Haitian Army who would have been next in line to assume the presidency under the Haitian Constitution if Aristide were to be killed or incapacitated.

Mr. Malary attended law school in Port-au-Prince, received a master's degree from Howard University, and conducted Ph.D. coursework at George Washington University in Washington, DC. He was a member of the International Law Association and counsel to the Central Bank of Haiti. He previously served as counsel to the US Agency for International Development (AID) in Haiti. There has been no investigation into his murder.

KESNER ODEUS ASSAULTED

On the night of July 4, 1993, Kesner Odéus, a judge in the civil court of St. Louis du Sud in Southern Haiti, was attacked by six armed men. Judge Odéus and his wife were both beaten and their house was destroyed. Although Judge Odéus never received a formal letter of dismissal, a new judge was appointed to his post after the attack.

GASTON TANIS ATTACKED, THREATENED

In October 1993, Gaston Tanis, a Justice of the Peace in Thiotte, in southeastern Haiti, was threatened by soldiers and armed civilians who accused him of being a confidant of President Aristide. On the night of October 22, Mr. Tanis was shot at and his house damaged after he refused to resign his post. (See also the case of Robert Cassagnol, above.)

HONDURAS

LINDA RIVERA LOBO THREATENED

Linda Rivera Lobo, an attorney and former criminal judge in the Honduran capital, Tegucigalpa, learned of a plot to assassinate her in May, 1993. Ms. Rivera had been the prosecuting attorney in the widely publicized case of Riccy Mabel Martínez Sevilla, a 17-year-old law student who was raped and murdered in July 1991. A former colonel named Castillo Maradiaga was convicted of homicide and rape and sentenced to 16 years in prison.

On May 22, 1993, Ms. Rivera learned from a reporter for Channel 6 television that Castillo Maradiaga had instigated a plot on her life. Col. Castillo had hired René Alemán, a soldier he had commanded in the Army's Communications Battalion, to assassinate Ms. Rivera. Alemán later admitted the colonel's offer to Ms. Rivera and gave details of the murder plot to the Honduran press. Col. Castillo's conviction in the Martínez Sevilla case is now being appealed by both the defense and the prosecution, which has asked for a heavier sentence.

MARCELINO MARTINEZ HARASSED, THREATENED

Marcelino Martínez, president and legal representative of the San Pedro Sula office of the Committee for the Defense of Human Rights in Honduras (CODEH), received repeated death threats at his office and home during the month of February, 1993. He reported threats at his office on February 12, 13, 15, 16 and 17 by an unidentified male who told him each time that he was going to die. Mr. Martínez's wife answered calls on February 15, 17, 18 and 19 at their home, where a female voice threatened her husband, herself and their four-year-old son. On February 18 they received a total of 12 calls between 5:00 and 8:00 pm, when they disconnected their phone.

During this same period Mr. Martínez was repeatedly followed by unknown men, one of whom rode a red motorcycle. He was also followed three times by an agent of the Honduran intelligence service, the National Directorate of Investigations (*Dirección Nacional de Investigaciones*, or DNI), a force that has frequently been implicated in human rights violations. At about the same time, the offices of CODEH in San Pedro Sula were broken into by unidentified burglars who apparently had master keys. Several crucial documents and photo negatives were stolen. At the time of these incidents, Mr. Martínez and CODEH were investigating the case of Eduardo Piña Van Tuyl, a businessman murdered on January 29, 1993, allegedly by members of the armed forces. The soldiers accused of the crime were subsequently acquitted.

MARIA ANTONIETA MENDOZA DE CASTRO THREATENED

Maria Antonieta Mendoza de Castro, Judge of the Second Criminal Court, received a death threat from an anonymous caller after pronouncing guilty verdicts against two members of the military, Col. Angel Sastillo Maradiaga and Sgt. Santos Eusebio Iovares Fúñez. The Lawyers Committee has not been able to confirm the date of the incident.

ANTONIO ZELAYA REYES THREATENED

Antonio Zelaya Reyes, representative of CODEH in the department of Olancho, reported in October 1993 that he had been repeatedly harassed and threatened by an unidentified man he believes to be connected with the police. The threats came after Mr. Zelaya denounced human rights abuses in the city of Catacamas on his regular radio program on Radio Catacamas. As reported in the 1992 edition of *In Defense of Rights*, Mr. Zelaya had previously been threatened at gunpoint by a police officer at the studio of Radio Catacamas.

MEXICO

SUSANA CODINA ATTACKED, HARASSED

Susana Codina is a labor lawyer representing two workers laid off by the Ford Motor Company. Even before the case came to court, Ms. Codina reported receiving threats at her home. On September 9, 1993, when the case came to trial, a gang entered the courtroom, shoved and verbally abused Ms. Codina, and beat the two defendants. The assailants were accompanied by a large group from the pro-government Federation of Mexican Workers (Confederación de Trabajadores de México, or CTM) No charges have been brought against Ms. Codina's attackers and no legal action has been taken to protect the lawyer or her clients.

JOEL GARCIA HARASSED

Joel García is a labor lawyer in the State of Tabasco. During 1993 he was involved in two controversial cases and was subsequently subjected to unfounded accusations and pressures from the state authorities. In the first case, Mr. García was representing the interests of 100 of 300 workers fired by the Mexican Oil Company, PEMEX. The case was resolved in their favor, and compensation was rewarded. In the second case, Mr. García was representing Aquiles Magaña, a well-known advocate for workers' rights in Tabasco. Mr. Magaña was charged with damaging public property during a demonstration by sanitation workers. Although he did not personally cause the damage, he was held accountable by the state and accused of being the intellectual author of the crime.

When Mr. García was rewarded with a percentage of the fee from the PEMEX case, the State of Tabasco charged him with fraud and issued a warrant for his arrest, arguing that it was illegal for him to charge a fee. Mr. García then took his case to a federal judge for review. The judge ruled that the charges were unfounded. The State of Tabasco responded by filing an appeal with the Supreme Court. The charges against Mr. García were eventually dismissed, but for the seven months that the arrest warrant remained in effect he was unable to enter the State of Tabasco. A colleague in his firm has speculated that the State pressed unfounded charges against Mr. García as a means of delaying his appeal on behalf of Mr. Magaña.

BARBARA ZAMORA LOPEZ HARASSED

Labor rights lawyer Barbara Zamora López has been repeatedly harassed and physically intimidated while trying to meet with and represent clients. In May 1993, in Chictalzingo in the State of Guerrero, Ms. Zamora was prevented from defending a group of indigenous clients charged with murder. The presiding judge, in a letter, promised to free the accused if they dismissed Ms. Zamora as their lawyer. Although the defendants did as the judge requested, they remained in detention.

In a separate incident, Ms. Zamora was pushed and physically harassed by prison security personnel when she attempted to visit two farmers detained in the State of Guerrero. She was also verbally abused by the commander of the prison, *Comandante* Gaspar Mirada. Although the case was brought before the state human rights commission, no action has been taken by Guerrero authorities to discipline those responsible or to offer Ms. Zamora protection.

NICARAGUA

LEONEL GONZALEZ VARGAS — KILLED

Leonel González Vargas, a Justice of the Peace and human rights advocate in the locality of La Batea in the Juigalpa region of central Nicaragua, was assassinated on March 24, 1993. According to the Nicaraguan Center for Human Rights (CENIDH), the killers dragged Mr. González from his home and shot him dead. Local press reports in *El Nuevo Diario* identified the gunmen as members of a group of rearmed rightist rebels known as *recontras*, under the command of a leader calling himself *Huracán* (Hurricane).

ITALO ANTINORI ASSAULTED, HARASSED THREATENED

Italo Antinori, a Panamanian lawyer specializing in constitutional law, was subjected to harassment, death threats and assault in various incidents in 1993. Mr. Antinori has acted on behalf of a group of citizens, including members of the Popular Alliance Party (*Partido Alianza Popular*) to bring criminal charges against Omaira Judith Correa Delgado, former mayor of Panama City. On March 26, 1993, Mr. Antinori filed charges against Ms. Correa with the Electoral Prosecutor of the Nation, accusing her of violations of Panama's electoral code by illegally using state resources to benefit the Popular Alliance Party. Additional charges were brought against Ms. Correa in April for violations of Articles 33 and 35 of the Panamanian Electoral Code.

Since filing these charges, according to the Centre for the Independence of Judges and Lawyers, Mr. Antinori has been repeatedly harassed and has received death threats from Ms. Correa and some of her associates. On April 28 and 29, during cross-examination of a witness in proceedings against her, Correa Delgado circulated notes in the courtroom with death threats against both the witness and Mr. Antinori.

On May 21, as Mr. Antinori was leaving his office with some colleagues, he was alerted to the presence of a man--later identified as a former member of the Panamanian air force--who was waiting for him in a brown car with a machine gun pointed out of the window. Mr. Antinori immediately returned to his office and alerted the police and the media. Men in two other cars parked nearby threatened reporters when they arrived, and one journalist was reportedly struck on the head with the butt of a gun. When the police arrived, the suspects rapidly fled the scene. They were apprehended shortly afterward and handguns and automatic weapons were confiscated. The men admitted to working for Correa Delgado.

PERU

HERIBERTO BENITEZ RIVAS — THREATENED

Heriberto Benítez Rivas, a lawyer involved in at least two high-profile and politically sensitive cases, has received anonymous death threats against himself and his family. The threats began in November 1992, when Mr. Benítez assumed the defense of army officers convicted of participating in a coup attempt earlier that year against the government of President Alberto Fujimori. The threats grew more frequent after May 1993, when Mr. Benítez undertook the representation of the relatives of nine students and one professor who were abducted on July 18, 1992 from the campus of the Enrique Guzmán y Valle University, also known as *La Cantuta*, allegedly by a division of the Peruvian Army. The ten were never seen alive again.

The *La Cantuta* case has achieved notoriety in Peru and internationally on account of the high government officials allegedly implicated, the government's failure to investigate the case, and the improbability of the accused receiving an impartial trial. At the time of the abduction, the campus was under the control of the army, on the belief that operations of the Shining Path insurgency (*Sendero Luminoso*) were being carried out there. Nevertheless, the army vigorously denied that it had detained the students and the professor. In April 1993, Peruvian Congressman Henry Pease made public a letter, purportedly written by a dissident faction of the army, which claimed that the students and the professor had been killed by a unit of the Army Intelligence Service (*Servicio de Inteligencia del Ejército*), with the knowledge of senior government officials including Vladimiro Montesinos, a close adviser to President Fujimori. A second letter, also purportedly written by the same dissident faction, was sent to the press. It contained a map showing the location of the remains of those who had disappeared. Using the map as a guide, a Peruvian magazine editor and forensic experts discovered bodies which appeared to have been shot in the head at close range. They also found personal belongings of the *La Cantuta* students, including keys that opened the school locker and house of one of those who had disappeared. As of December 31, 1993, parallel proceedings in the case were underway under civilian and military jurisdiction.

Given the political sensitivity of the *La Cantuta* case, the death threats against Mr. Benítez were of particular concern. On September 14, 1993, after he had notified the Lima Bar Association and the Congressional Committee on Human Rights about the threats, the National Police Command provided Mr. Benítez with special protection; by early December, however, this had been discontinued. Mr. Benítez was also told that there was an outstanding detention order against him, but was never informed of the charges. Once again he filed complaints with the Lima Bar Association and the Congressional Committee on Human Rights, fearing that he would be the target of an assassination attempt.

MANUEL ROSAS BURE CAMACHO DETAINED, HARASSED

Many of the attacks on Peruvian lawyers described below, such as that of Manuel Rosas Bure Camacho, occurred in the context of the Peruvian government's efforts to combat terrorism, which has claimed the lives of thousands of Peruvians since 1980. In many cases, however, these efforts have failed to conform to international human rights standards. Overly broad laws, and largely unfettered police discretion in enforcing them, have cast a broad net of suspicion over Peruvian society, entangling many individuals including lawyers without the benefit of due process.

On April 5, 1992, President Fujimori suspended the Peruvian Constitution, claiming that it was ineffective in countering the terrorist onslaught. Shortly thereafter he issued executive decrees nos. 25475 and 25659, the Anti-Terrorism and Treason decrees. These greatly expanded the definitions of terrorism and treason, while abolishing or severely restricting procedural safeguards in the trials of such offenses. Cases are tried by anonymous "faceless judges" (*jueces sin rostro*), who conduct proceedings covered by a hood or seated behind a one-way mirror. Proceedings are not open to the public, and many times the defense counsel is not shown the case record until a few hours before the trial begins. Police do not appear as witnesses, so there is no opportunity to rebut the allegations contained in their reports, which form the primary — and often the only — basis for the prosecution.

Lawyer Manuel Rosas Bure Camacho was charged under Peru's Anti-Terrorism decrees as a result of his defense of eleven peasants charged as terrorists in November 1992 in Lambayeque in northern Peru. The case, which received a large amount of publicity, highlighted the lack of procedural guarantees under the decrees, and the police's harsh treatment of those accused but not yet convicted of terrorism.

The peasants and Mr. Bure formed part of the Committee to Defend the Forest of San Ignacio (*Comité de Defensa de los Bosques de San Ignacio*), which sought to preserve the forest from development. The eleven peasants were detained in June 1992 after a bomb explosion killed two people at a company involved in the commercial exploitation of forest resources.

Some of the peasants were reportedly tortured in prison and Mr. Bure was repeatedly harassed in the course of representing the detainees. In October 1992, Mr. Bure himself was detained and charged with terrorism, based on confidential information given to the police, reportedly by the company. In March 1993 the peasants were acquitted due to lack of evidence. Mr. Bure was also acquitted and released after spending more than four months in prison.

LUCIO CUADRA GONZALEZ INDICTED

As reported in the 1992 edition of *In Defense of Rights*, Lucio Cuadra González, a lawyer in the northern department of Cajamarca, was detained and indicted under the Anti-Terrorism decrees in November 1992, based on allegations which a court had previously dismissed for lack of evidence. In 1991, Santos Gilberto Robles Paredes, who was accused of terrorism, had accused Mr. Cuadra of belonging to *Sendero Luminoso* and of trying to recruit local peasants.

However, the charges had been dropped when Mr. Robles recanted his accusation, saying that police had extracted it under torture. The 1992 charges were improperly brought, since the Anti-Terrorism decrees do not apply to prior acts. Nevertheless, Mr. Cuadra was tried before a faceless judge in June 1993. During the month-long trial, Mr. Robles admitted that he did not know Mr. Cuadra and that his testimony had been coerced by a National Police colonel. In July 1993, the faceless judge ruled that there were serious deficiencies in the police investigation of the case and acquitted Mr. Cuadra of all charges. He was released after spending some seven months in detention.

JAMES GAGEL INDICTED

As reported in the 1992 edition of *In Defense of Rights*, lawyer James Gagel, a US citizen who arranged adoptions of Peruvian infants by families in the United States, was arrested at his home on February 24, 1992. He faced a number of charges, including kidnapping and trafficking in children, forgery of documents and impersonating an official. The case against Mr. Gagel was fraught with procedural irregularities, including the criminal judge's frequent *ex parte* communications with the prosecutor, interviews with the press regarding confidential proceedings, and lack of access to evidence and attendance at hearings by Mr. Gagel, who was acting in his own defense. US Embassy officials in Lima concluded that the charges were false and the result of a frame-up.

In August 1993, the criminal chamber of the Peruvian Supreme Court removed the case to a different court, based on the irregularities in the lower court. The Supreme Court also noted that the trial court had improperly determined Mr. Gagel's guilt before hearing any evidence. A new trial was scheduled to begin on October 15, 1993; however, hearing dates were postponed and the trial never commenced. On December 31, 1993, a new judge was appointed to the case, but a trial date had yet to be scheduled. Mr. Gagel remains on provisional liberty and may not leave Peru.

EMMA VIGUERAS MINAYA HARASSED

Lawyer Emma Vigueras Minaya has been repeatedly harassed while representing persons charged with offenses under the Anti-Terrorism decrees. While representing a client, Pablo Rojas Tamayo, on a charge of treason, she was constantly followed by police. On July 24, 1993, unidentified individuals forcefully tried to prevent her from filing an appeal on behalf of Juan Alonso Aranda Company, who had been convicted of treason. On August 24, 1993, a police officer interrupted a court appearance by Ms. Vigueras in a case related to that of *La Cantuta* (see above). (Ms. Vigueras was representing the Dean of the Enrique Guzmán y Valle University against charges of abuse of authority.) The police officer attempted to halt the proceeding by threatening Ms. Vigueras in open court; when this did not succeed, he detained a personal guard of the Dean who was also in court. The guard was released after five hours in detention, during which time he heard the police officer accuse Ms. Vigueras of belonging to the Association of Democratic Lawyers (*Asociación de Abogados Democráticos*). (see below)

Ms. Vigueras notified the Lima Bar Association of these episodes of harassment. The Bar Association in turn filed complaints with the Peruvian Ministry of the Interior, the Inter-American Commission on Human Rights of the Organization of American States and the General Secretariat of the United Nations. On August 12, 1993, members of the National Anti-Terrorism Police (DINCOTE) went to Ms. Vigueras' house at night and served her with a request to testify as to her complaints before these organizations. This constitutes further harassment of Ms. Vigueras, since DINCOTE is only empowered to investigate cases of terrorism and treason.

ASSOCIATION OF DEMOCRATIC LAWYERS HARASSED

LAWYER-TO-LAWYER NETWORK APPEAL,
FEBRUARY 1993

The *Asociación de Abogados Democráticos* (ADL) is a group of lawyers who frequently defend persons accused of committing terrorist acts on behalf of *Sendero Luminoso*. The Peruvian government has often denounced members of the group as active participants in the insurgency. In 1992, following President Fujimori's suspension of the Constitution and enactment of the Anti-Terrorist decrees, a number of these lawyers were charged for terrorist actions. These cases were described in the 1992 edition of *In Defense of Rights*.

In May 1993, members of the ADL brought a complaint against the Peruvian government before the Inter-American Commission on Human Rights. Included in the complaint were several of the lawyers listed below; none was identified, however, as belonging to the ADL. Indeed, some of the lawyers mentioned in the complaint deny any association with this group, as noted below. The complaint alleges that the Peruvian government has violated the rights of these lawyers, including their right to life; to equality under the law; to the presumption of innocence; to freedom of thought, conscience, association and expression; and to freedom to work in their chosen field.

ALFREDO CRESPO BRAGAYRAC IMPRISONED

Lawyer Alfredo Crespo Bragayrac represented *Sendero Luminoso* leader Abimael Guzmán after his capture in September 1992. Crespo was himself detained on January 11, 1993 and charged with treason, based on allegations that he was a member of *Sendero* and had engaged in the logistics of terrorist acts, before and after the capture of Guzmán. He was tried summarily, according to the same laws and procedures applied against Guzmán, and was sentenced to life imprisonment by a faceless judge on January 27, 1993. On the same day, his colleague Jorge Cartagena Vargas, was also convicted on similar charges (see below). Under the Anti-Terrorist decrees, both proceedings were held in secret. After the convictions of Mr. Crespo and Mr. Cartagena, the Lima Bar Association, Peru's most influential lawyers group, publicly objected to the secret proceedings, on the ground that, if the incriminating evidence included the lawyers' representation of convicted terrorists, the right to be represented by a lawyer would be seriously compromised:

> The Association expresses its concern that two lawyers have been sentenced to life imprisonment, and that proof of their participation in acts constituting terrorism or treason has not been made public. The public disclosure of this proof is indispensable in these cases because both professionals were defending terrorists. If their convictions were in any way linked

to their defense work, this would constitute a flagrant violation of the right of defense.

JORGE CARTAGENA VARGAS IMPRISONED

Jorge Cartagena represented Marta Huatay, Osmán Morote and other alleged leaders of *Sendero Luminoso.* In July 1992, he was shot in his office, reportedly by members of the rightist paramilitary *Comando Rodrigo Franco.* On January 11, 1993, he was detained on charges of treason. As in the case of Alfredo Crespo Bragayrac, police alleged that he was actively involved in planning terrorist actions both before and after the capture of Abimael Guzmán. Mr. Cartagena was summarily tried, convicted and sentenced to life imprisonment on January 27, 1993.

ANDRES COELLO DETAINED

Lawyer Andrés Coello was also detained on January 11, 1993, on charges of treason. He was alleged by anti-terrorism police to be a member of the ADL in Lima. However, he was released after two days for lack of evidence.

The eight lawyers whose cases are described below are all from the Chiclayo area of northern Peru. Several of them were detained during a wave of arrests of more than 40 people in Chiclayo during November and December 1992 on charges of either terrorism or treason.

ERNESTO ANSELMO CUBAS MONTES INDICTED

Ernesto Anselmo Cubas Montes was detained on December 3, 1992 at his law office in Chiclayo and charged with terrorism. The police record in his case states that he defended persons accused of terrorism and of belonging to either *Sendero Luminoso* or the *Movimiento Revolucionario Túpac Amaru* (MRTA), Peru's other main insurgent group. Mr. Cubas was also charged with seeking to organize an ADL group in Chiclayo, and with recruiting four other lawyers for that purpose, including Gilver Alarcón Requejo, Victor Renán Sigueñas Campos, Rubén Bustamante Banda and Miguel Olazábal Ancajima (see below). His record further states that he acknowledged belonging to *Socorro Popular*, a group linked to *Sendero Luminoso*. Mr. Cubas reportedly denied all of these charges by police on the ground that his statements had been extracted under torture and as the result of threats against his family. At the end of 1993, Mr. Cubas was awaiting trial by a faceless judge.

GILVER (or GILMER) ALARCON REQUEJO INDICTED

Lawyer Gilver Alarcón Requejo was charged with terrorism as a result of the police interrogation of Ernesto Cubas. According to police reports, he is alleged to be a local leader of *Sendero Luminoso*, and had documents in his office which police say establish his association with the insurgent group. Mr. Alarcón was not detained and was being tried *in absentia*, as permitted by legislation in force at the time. Through his lawyer, Mr. Alarcón denied the accusation, arguing that the writings found in his office were public documents which he used for his university classes and thesis research. On November 25, 1993, the Anti-Terrorist legislation was amended and trials *in absentia* were disallowed. His case was due to come before a faceless judge in 1994.

VICTOR RENAN SIGUENAS CAMPOS INDICTED

Lawyer Victor Renán Sigueñas Campos was detained on December 17, 1992, also based on the statements of Ernesto Cubas. The police also asserted that, while Mr. Sigueñas did not have subversive literature or materials in his possession, he allegedly had the business cards of other members of the ADL. Mr. Sigueñas denied having any association with the group and claimed that the police had arrested him in reprisal for having won dismissals of terrorism charges against several individuals. His case was due to come before a faceless judge in 1994.

RUBEN BUSTAMANTE BANDA INDICTED

Lawyer Rubén Bustamante Banda was detained in his law offices on December 7, 1992. The police record in his case stated that he was the head of the ADL in the Chiclayo area and a leader of *Sendero Luminoso*. The police also alleged that they found subversive literature in his possession. Mr. Bustamante denied the allegations, stating that his detention was designed to punish him for having filed a writ of habeas corpus against certain officers of the anti-terrorist police (DINCOTE) in relation to a case he was defending. Mr. Bustamante further stated that the allegedly subversive writings from *Sendero Luminoso* were used in his litigation research to defend cases under Peruvian anti-terrorist legislation. His case was set to come before a faceless judge in early 1994.

MIGUEL OLAZABAL ANCAJIMA — INDICTED

Lawyer Miguel Olazábal Ancajima was detained on December 7, 1992. He was shown to the press on December 15, 1992, wearing a striped prison uniform, and declared to be a terrorist. He was not, however, charged until the following day. The police record in his case stated that he was a member of both the ADL and *Socorro Popular*. It also alleged that a document was found in his possession containing the names of two persons charged with treason under Anti-Terrorism decrees. Mr. Olazábal's indictment improperly commented that both his brother and brother-in-law had been accused of treason. His case was set to come before a faceless judge in early 1994.

CARLOS ANTONIO HONORES IGLESIAS — INDICTED

Police detained Carlos Antonio Honores Iglesias at his law office in the northern city of Trujillo on November 10, 1993 and charged him with treason. He was taken to the Picsi Prison in nearby Chiclayo. The police alleged that an accused terrorist in Chiclayo had named Mr. Honores as a member of *Sendero Luminoso*; they further alleged that subversive materials had been found in his office. Mr. Honores reportedly acknowledged his membership in the ADL in the early 1980s, but denied any current involvement with the lawyers' group or with *Sendero Luminoso*. Mr. Honores has represented individuals accused of terrorism and has won acquittals in some cases. The Bar Associations of Chiclayo, La Libertad and Lambayeque have all stated their belief in Mr. Honores' innocence and demanded that he be granted a fair and impartial trial.

ABSALON RIOS CABALLERO
OSCAR CIEZA DIAZ DETAINED

Police detained Chiclayo lawyers Absalón Ríos Caballero and Oscar Cieza Díaz in mid-November 1993 and searched their offices. Their detention was based upon incriminating testimony that alleged them to be members of the ADL. In representing a number of accused terrorists, the testimony added, Mr. Ríos and Mr. Cieza Díaz were following orders from *Sendero Luminoso* to obstruct justice, impede the actions of the police and security forces, and obtain the release of imprisoned terrorists.

Both lawyers have denied the charges against them. Mr. Ríos has said that he was appointed by the Lambayeque Bar Association to represent Gilver Alarcón Requejo (see above). The police search of Mr. Ríos' office did not uncover any incriminating evidence; in addition, the incriminating testimony against him has been discredited due to several factual inaccuracies. Mr. Cieza Díaz has similarly claimed that he represented accused terrorists not on orders from *Sendero Luminoso*, but on the request of the Superior Court, the Bar Association of Lambayeque or relatives of the accused. His testimony has been corroborated by court records, testimony from the Dean of the Lambayeque Bar Association and relatives of defendants accused on terrorism charges. Despite the indications of their innocence, both Mr. Ríos and Mr. Cieza Díaz remain in jail.

UNIVERSIDAD NACIONAL DE SAN MARCOS LAW SCHOOL
BELIA BERROCAL TITO
CARLOS DELGADO ALTAMIRANO
ARTURO ENCARNACION NIETO
CARLOS ISLA LITARDO
GERARDO MUNARRIZ ULLOA
ANGEL PEREZ BONETT
PEDRO VALDES BERNALES INDICTED

These seven students and graduates of the Law School of the Universidad Nacional de San Marcos in Lima were detained on November 18-19, 1992 and charged with terrorism. All seven were tried in a single action based upon similar evidence. In each case, the police claimed that the accused were in possession of subversive pamphlets and books; the accused denied having them and asserted that they had been planted by the police. The police also charged that their names appeared on scraps of paper discovered in the office of Marta Huatay, an attorney convicted of treason for participating in terrorist activities organized by *Sendero Luminoso*. The police alleged that this evidence showed that the accused belonged to the legal defense section of *Socorro Popular*. The seven were acquitted of all charges on August 20, 1993, after spending nine months in jail.

TRINIDAD AND TOBAGO

REGINALD ARMOUR
GREGORY DALZIN
CHRISTOPHER HAMEL-SMITH

DOUGLAS MENDEZ THREATENED

LAWYER-TO-LAWYER NETWORK APPEAL, NOVEMBER 1993

Reginald Armour, secretary of the Trinidad and Tobago Law Association, and three other lawyers received anonymous threatening phone calls, including death threats, between August 21-23, 1993. The calls came in response to their efforts to stop the executions of two clients who had been convicted of murder and sentenced to death by hanging. In an attempt to halt the executions, which were scheduled for August 24, the four lawyers filed constitutional motions before the High Court, appealing the finality of the verdicts and the death sentences. Their motions cited the extended time that the prisoners had spent on death row as "cruel and unusual punishment" (one had been sentenced in 1983, the other in 1988).

On August 21, at a local conference of the ruling People's National Movement, National Security Minister Russell Huggins made an inflammatory appeal to party activists to protest any attempt to overturn the two prisoners' death sentences. "In this country," Mr. Huggins said, "certain persons are overly concerned with protecting the rights of the criminal....So on Monday, when they file their motions to stop the hangings, you must get up and let your voices be heard." The Minister added that the lawyers' actions were frustrating the functioning of the executive branch and the State's right to impose capital punishment. His remarks contravened the right of Trinidadian lawyers to exercise their professional duties freely, as guaranteed under domestic law by the Legal Profession Act of 1986. In addition, Principle 16 of the UN Basic Principles on the Role of Lawyers (see appendix) states that: "Governments shall ensure that lawyers...are able to perform all of their professional functions without intimidation, hindrance, harassment or improper interference."

After the Minister's speech, the four lawyers received a stream of obscene and threatening telephone calls. Mr. Hamel-Smith was told, "We are coming to lynch you." Despite these threats, which were apparently incited by Mr. Huggins' speech, the lawyers went ahead with their motion on August 23 and a stay of execution was granted.

VENEZUELA

BRAULIO SANCHEZ THREATENED

Braulio Sánchez, judge of the 26th Penal Court of First Instance, was threatened with arrest by Venezuela's military courts for "abuse of power" and "interfering with military justice." This confrontation developed between the military judiciary and Judge Sánchez over a habeas corpus order he had issued in the trial of a number of individuals charged with rebellion in connection with the failed military coup attempt of November 27, 1992. The Venezuelan Supreme Court had declared unconstitutional the special military courts used to try the accused rebels and had remanded the cases to the ordinary military courts, which failed to file formal charges within the statutory time limits.

On March 26 and 29, 1993, Judge Sánchez issued writs of habeas corpus, granting a hearing to those individuals still in military custody but not charged in a timely manner. On March 30, the military courts refused to produce the prisoners and issued a warrant for Judge Sánchez's arrest. Judge Sánchez's writ was affirmed, however, by Judge Luís Lecuna of the 19th Superior Penal Court. Judge Sánchez, in turn, opened a case against the president of the Military Court for ignoring his order. Civilian judges went on strike for two days in support of their colleague, and the tense confrontation was only defused when the Supreme Court agreed to decide the jurisdictional issues at the request of the Judicial Council, the governing body of Venezuela's civlian judges. By the end of the year, the Supreme Court had yet to rule on the dispute, while the trials of most of the accused rebels before the special military courts had concluded.

GONZALO RODRIGUEZ CORRO ATTACKED, THREATENED

Gonzalo Rodríguez Corro, President of the Supreme Court of Venezuela, received a letter-bomb at his home on July 19, 1993. It was defused by police. On the same day a similar letter-bomb was delivered by a mail carrier to the building that houses the Supreme Court, where it exploded, blowing off the left hand of a court employee. A number of other members of the Court reported receiving threats, and additional bomb threats were received at the Supreme Court building during the remainder of July.

The Venezuelan government launched an investigation into the attacks and threats. Press speculation about the motive for the attacks focussed on the pending proceedings in the Supreme Court against then-President Carlos Andrés Pérez and former President Jaime Lusinchi for corruption. (Justice Corro was the magistrate responsible for writing the Court's decision in the Pérez case). The press also concluded that it was likely military or police forces had been the source for the sophisticated explosives used in the letter-bombs.

On August 8, 1993 the police arrested a former commissioner of the intelligence police of the Interior Ministry, the *Dirección de los Servicios de Inteligencia y Prevención* (DISIP), and charged him with fabrication of the bombs. Another former DISIP agent was arrested on August 13, and others were also implicated. Both men arrested had extensive ties to the Venezuelan security forces and to both of the former presidents on trial for corruption. After the arrests, the attacks on the Court ceased. The cases have yet to come to trial and little additional information concerning the intellectual authorship of the attacks has come to light.

MIDDLE EAST

BRAHIM TAOUTI IMPRISONED

LAWYER-TO-LAWYER NETWORK
APPEAL, FEBRUARY 1993

On May 3, 1993, the Military Tribunal of Blida convicted lawyer Brahim Taouti of "possession and distribution of documents harmful to the national interest," in violation of Article 96 of the Penal Code. He was sentenced to the maximum penalty of three years' imprisonment.Maître Taouti's "offense"--to which he freely admitted--was to have received from his client, Islamic Salvation Front (FIS) leader Ali Belhadj, a 174-page document, and to have distributed that document to two other members of the FIS defense team, as well as to the Algerian League for Human Rights (LADH), the Algerian League for the Defense of Human Rights (LADDH), and the governmental National Observatory for Human Rights. The document, a commentary on the political situation in Algeria by Mr. Belhadj, was handed to Maître Taouti during a visit to his client at Blida Military prison on December 23, 1992, in the presence of the prison director and his assistant.

His arrest on February 2, 1993 prevented Maître Taouti from appearing in a February 16 appeal hearing for Mr. Belhadj before the Supreme Court. Maître Taouti was held in preventive detention at Blida Military Prison from the day of his arrest until his trial, even though Algeria's Code of Criminal Procedure limits pre-trial detention to use only in exceptional cases. Defense lawyers allege that he was mistreated during this period, that his hair and beard were shaved and that he was held in solitary confinement.

His trial before a military court was unfair. It took place in a military base with no public access, and before a tribunal that lacked independence from the executive branch. The government did not reply to repeated requests by the Lawyers Committee and Middle East watch to observe the trial. The prosecution based its case on the contention that extracts from Mr. Belhadj's statement had appeared on the walls of mosques, and had incited violence against the authorities. However, no evidence was presented to implicate Maître Taouti in the public dissemination of the document, beyond having shared it with lawyers and human rights organizations.

The action for which Brahim Taouti was convicted is in accord with the usual professional duties of lawyers. The document he distributed to lawyers and human rights organizations was clearly of legitimate interest at a time when lawyers were preparing a joint case for an appeal hearing. The legislation under which he was convicted is excessively broad, to the extent that it endangers the right to freedom of expression. Maître Taouti appears to have been imprisoned for no reason other than his active defense of clients unpopular with the government.

ALI ZOUITA DETAINED

LAWYER-TO-LAWYER NETWORK
APPEAL, FEBRUARY 1993

Lawyer Ali Zouita was detained on February 1, 1993, on suspicion of having disseminated subversive documents from another imprisoned FIS leader, Abdelkader Hachani. His detention took place prior to his scheduled appearance before the Supreme Court as part of a team of lawyers representing FIS leaders in an appeal against their prison sentences. According to defense lawyers, after arrest Maître Zouita was taken for interrogation to Châteauneuf Police Station, where he was held for 13 days and allegedly subjected to torture. Following this, he was accused of other offenses including membership of an armed subversive movement, incitement to murder and involvement in the escape from prison of FIS leader, Rabah Kebir. Maître Zouita did not come to trial on these serious offenses during 1993. He is currently held in Serkadji Prison in the capital, Algiers.

ALGERIAN LEGAL PROFESSION HARASSED

Algeria's descent into armed confrontation between the military government and the FIS and its supporters, since the cancellation of elections in January 1991, has devastated the Algerian justice system. Military courts, which had given up their jurisdiction over civilians in 1989, were reactivated after January 1991, detracting from the competence of the civilian judiciary.

Sweeping new anti-terrorism laws, passed in September 1992, essentially prohibited all criticism of the government. The new laws provided for the creation of Special Courts, with civilian judges appointed by the President of the Republic. In April 1993, the anti-terrorism laws were further strengthened to give Special Court judges powers to expel or suspend lawyers who "use dilatory and obstructionist maneuvers" when appearing before them. Lawyers presenting a vigorous defense before the Special Courts, where international fair trial standards were already violated by virtue of the executive's direct appointment of judges, therefore risked suspension from the legal profession for periods of up to a year.

Algerian lawyers protested this interference with their ability to carry out their professional duties, and branch meetings of the Algerian Bar Association in Annaba, Batna, Constantine and Algiers resolved to boycott the Special Courts until these measures were suspended. The government declared these meetings illegal, however, commenting implausibly that, "These debates are not the prerogatives of general assemblies of lawyers, because they are not of a professional nature." On May 10, 1993 the government obtained a ruling from the administrative chamber of the Supreme Court, placing an injunction on the implementation of any resolution to boycott the Special Courts by a bar association branch.

For the remainder of 1993, lawyers complied grudgingly with the Supreme Court ruling. For example, in the Special Court trial of 58 people accused of placing a bomb at Boumédienne International Airport, members of the defense team either absented themselves from hearings or appeared late, until threatened with suspension and even imprisonment by the President of the Court under the amended anti-terrorism law. After this, they participated in the proceedings. In one case, a judge in Algiers ordered the suspension of eleven lawyers, but the order was lifted after the intervention of the Algiers branch of the bar association. Otherwise, no actual suspensions of lawyers were reported in 1993.

ALGERIAN JUDGES AND PROSECUTORS KILLED

More than 500 suspected supporters of the Islamist opposition were killed by the security forces in 1993. At the same time, at least 200 killings were attributed to armed groups believed to be supporters of the FIS. The dead included at least seven judges and prosecutors. FIS leaders abroad issued equivocal statements about this campaign of violence, which targeted unarmed civilians as well as members of the Algerian security forces. The Lawyers Committee condemned all killings of civilians by armed opposition groups, as well as other killings which violated international human rights law.

The assassinated judges and magistrates included:

MAHFOUZ BEKAI	President of the Blida Military Court, assassinated June 15, 1993.
MAHFOUZ KERDALI	46-year-old *juge d'instruction* (investigating magistrate) from Algiers, killed November 30, 1993.
LAKHDAR ROUAZ	President of the Special Court of Oran Killed December 6, 1993.
CHIEF PROSECUTOR TLEMCEN SPECIAL COURT	no details available
PRESIDENT, KOLEA SPECIAL COURT	no details available
ASSISTANT PROSECUTOR ALGIERS SPECIAL COURT	no details available
PRESIDENT TENES SPECIAL COURT	no details available

AHMED HAMBALI — KILLED

Several legal scholars are also known to have been killed in Algeria's recent wave of political violence. The only case in which details are available, however, is that of Ahmed Hambali, professor of Islamic Law at the University of Tizi Ouzou. Professor Hambali, who was known for his attempts to mediate in the confrontation between the government and its Islamist opponents, was shot dead by a group of hooded gunmen on September 30, 1993. Those responsible have not been identified.

EGYPT

TAREK METWALI AHMED — DETAINED

Lawyer Tarek Metwali Ahmed was among the accused in the case of the Vanguards of Conquest IV. The Vanguards of Conquest are an Islamist organization that has resorted to arms in its effort to overthrow the Egyptian government. Members of the organization were split into four groups for trial and tried in September-October 1993 in proceedings that involved hundreds of defendants. Mr. Ahmed was detained in July 1993 at a time when he was acting as a defense lawyer for a number of prisoners from the group. He was acquitted on October 30, 1993, but has remained in administrative detention. Emergency legislation continuously in force in Egypt since 1981 permits administrative detention for up to 90 days. After that time, any extension should be authorized by a judge. However, the Ministry of the Interior often overrides court orders to release administrative detainees, holding them in detention indefinitely.

NIZAR MAHMOUD GHURAB DETAINED

On October 30, 1993, lawyer Nizar Mahmoud Ghurab was acquitted of involvement in the Vanguards of Conquest. Despite his acquittal, Mr. Ghurab has remained in administrative detention without charge or trial. He was arrested in June 1993, at a time when he was acting as a defense attorney for a number of defendants from the Vanguards of Conquest I group.

AHMED MUHAMMAD HAREIDI DETAINED

Lawyer Ahmed Muhammad Hareidi was arrested in March 1992 and accused of involvement in politically motivated acts of violence in the town of Dairut in Upper Egypt. Despite being acquitted of these charges on December 30, 1992, he remained in administrative detention.

MUHAMMAD SAYED EID HASSANEIN DETAINED

Muhammad Sayed Eid Hassanein, a lawyer, was detained in February 1993. He was held at first as a hostage for his brother, who was wanted in connection with acts of violence perpetrated by an illegal political group. It is common for the Egyptian authorities to hold family members of wanted suspects from such groups in order to encourage the suspects to give themselves up. Mr. Hassanein was charged with the same offenses as his brother, but was acquitted. Nevertheless, he has remained in detention despite numerous court orders for his release.

MUSTAFA MUHAMMAD AL-IRAQI DETAINED

Lawyer Mustafa Muhammad al-Iraqi was acquitted of involvement in the Islamist al-Shawqiyun organization on August 21, 1993. Al-Shawqiyun had resorted to violence in order to overthrow the Egyptian government, and 24 of its members were convicted of involvement in four politically motivated murders, together with other offenses relating to the illegal possession of firearms and explosives. Four of them received the death sentence. Prior to his arrest, Mr. al-Iraqi had been engaged as a defense attorney by some of the defendants in this case. Despite his acquittal, he remained in administrative detention throughout the remainder of 1993.

MANSOUR AHMED MANSOUR DETAINED

Lawyer Mansour Ahmed Mansour remained in detention throughout 1993. He was arrested in July 1992 on charges of involvement in the assassination of the prominent writer Faraq Fouda. Mr. Mansour was acquitted in August 21, 1993, but has remained in administrative detention since then despite two court orders for his release.

MUHAMMED HELMI MURAD DETAINED

Dr. Murad, a 73-year-old lawyer and former government minister, writes for *ash-sha'ab*, the twice-weekly newspaper of the opposition Labor Party. According to Human Rights Watch/Middle East , Dr. Murad was detained and questioned in October 1993. The book *Why We Say No to Mubarak*, a collection of articles by Dr. Murad and Adil Hussein, was ordered confiscated on the grounds that it constituted "propaganda for extremist ideas and and a justification of terrorist organizations." According to the Egyptian Organization for Human Rights, the charges against Dr. Murad include "contempt of the person of the President of the Republic," under Article 98 of the Penal Code.

ZAKI ABDEL QADER RADWAN DETAINED

Zaki Abdel Qader Radwan, a lawyer active in the defense of prisoners from banned Islamist political groups, was detained in June 1993. He has remained in administrative detention since then, despite orders for his release at a number of court hearings.

NABAWI IBRAHIM AL-SAYED DETAINED

Lawyer Nabawi Ibrahim al-Sayed defended a number of those accused in the Vanguards of Conquest cases. Mr. al-Sayed was placed in administrative detention on the completion of the trial on October 30, 1993.

IBRAHIM ALI AL-SAYED DETAINED

Ibrahim Ali al-Sayed is a lawyer who has been active in the defense of accused members of politically violent groups. He was placed in administrative detention in October 1993. According to the Egyptian Organization for Human Rights (EOHR), Mr. al-Sayed had been warned by the governor of Shabeen al-Kom prison not to visit prisoners from violent groups, but had disregarded the warning.

HASSAN AL-GHARBAWI SHEHATA DETAINED

Cairo lawyer Hassan al-Gharbawi Shehata remained in administrative detention throughout 1993. Mr. Shehata was arrested in January 1989 and charged in connection with civil disturbances in the Ain Shams district of Cairo. He was acquitted of all charges in May 1990, but has remained in detention despite numerous court orders calling for his release. Prior to his arrest, Mr. Shehata had been active in defending suspected supporters of banned Islamist opposition groups.

RADWAN AL-TOUNI INDICTED
MUSTAFA AL-SAYYID ABD AL-'AAL

Radwan al-Touni is a lawyer in Asyut, a city in southern Egypt that has been a center of political violence between armed Islamist groups and the Egyptian security forces. Active in defending clients accused of membership in illegal Islamist opposition groups, Mr. al-Touni is Chair of the Civil Liberties' Committee of the Asyut Branch of the Egyptian Bar Association. He was detained under emergency legislation on December 5, 1992. After interrogation, he was charged with involvement in an extremist group accused of armed attacks on tourists. During March and April 1993, more than forty civilian defendants, including Mr. al-Touni, stood trial before a military court in proceedings that were judged unfair by a trial observer from the International Commission of Jurists. In addition to concerns that military courts have superseded the jurisdiction of the civilian judiciary, the defense lawyers in the case were given inadequate time to examine case documents and denied access to their clients until the case opened.

Mr. al-Touni was eventually acquitted and released from detention in April 1993. The Asyut Branch of the Egyptian Bar Association accused the authorities of wrongfully arresting Mr. al-Touni and a second Asyut lawyer, Mustafa al-Sayyid Abd al-'Aal, who was also tried and acquitted in the same case. It viewed their arrests as an attempt to discourage lawyers from representing defendants accused of involvement with outlawed Islamist opposition groups.

EGYPTIAN MILITARY JUDGES
GEN. MUHAMMAD ABDALLAH
GEN. MUHAMMAD WAJDI AL-LA'ATHI
GEN. IMAD ABDALLAH
GEN. ALI KAMAL HAMZAH
GEN. ABD-AL GHAFUR HILAL
GEN. FAYSAL HAYBAH
COL. SHAMAL RAMZI
LT. COL. MAHMOUD SULTAN THREATENED

During 1992, President Hosni Mubarak extended the jurisdiction of Egypt's military courts to cover crimes against internal security. Since then there has been a large increase in the number of death sentences and executions in Egypt. In their proceedings, the military courts have failed to comply with minimum international fair trial standards.

In November 1993, the Jihad (Holy War) group issued public death threats against these eight judges named above, who sit on military courts responsible for trying cases involving political violence by Islamist opposition groups. In a statement issued to international news agencies, Jihad asserted that the eight were responsible for sentencing to death 38 supporters of Islamist groups. The organization said that the judges were "apostates" because they had presided over trials that "violated Islamic law."

IRAQ

JASSEM MUKHLIS — KILLED

Seventy-two-year-old lawyer Jassem Mukhlis was one of dozens of senior Iraqi figures executed in late 1993 by the regime of President Saddam Hussein. Mr. Mukhlis, a former ambassador and a member of the most prominent family in the town of Tikrit, was detained by security agents at his Baghdad home on July 17, 1993. His brother, Sof'r Mukhlis, was detained at the same time and was also later executed. According to Human Rights Watch/Middle East and Amnesty International, the detentions and subsequent executions form part of a wider crackdown on alleged opponents of the regime from Iraq's Sunni Arab heartland. None of those executed was charged with any specific offense or afforded any form of legal proceeding. Mr. Mukhlis had no known connection to any Iraqi opposition group.

In November 1993, the detainees' relatives were summoned to the Baghdad offices of Special Security (*Amn al-Khas*), an elite intelligence agency run by the president's son, Qusai Hussein. They were told to go to the morgue to collect the corpses of their relatives. Each had been shot once behind the left ear. Official death certificates noted the cause of death as "heart attack." Relatives were forbidden to hold traditional burial cemeteries, or to make any public reference to the executions.

MOHAMMED MAHER SALEH EN-NAZLI ATTACKED

Gazan lawyer Mohammed Maher Saleh En-Nazli was seriously injured when Israeli soldiers opened fire on his car on November 3, 1993. According to the Gaza Center for Rights and Law, his son and neighbor were getting into the car when members of the Israeli Defense Forces opened fire on the vehicle at close range. Mohammed En-Nazli sustained serious injuries to his face and hand; his five-year-old son suffered minor injuries. The Gaza Bar Association reportedly declared a three-day strike from November 6-8 to protest the shooting. When the strike ended, lawyers were denied access to the military courts for several days. During this time cases went ahead without legal representation for defendants.

WALID FAHUM CLIENT ACCESS DENIED

Attorney Walid Fahum is a Palestinian citizen of Israel, chair of the Association for Prisoner Rehabilitation and a member of the Arab Association for Human Rights (HRA). On January 19, 1993, Mr. Fahum was denied access to a client in prison and was informed that the Prison Services had issued a one-year injunction prohibiting him from entering any prison.

The injunction was reportedly issued as a result of an incident on October 6, 1992, during a visit by Mr. Fahum to Palestinian political prisoners in Ashkelon prison who were conducting a hunger strike against their conditions. After a thorough search of Mr. Fahum's person and files, he was admitted to a room in which to meet his clients. In the course of his interviews, Mr. Fahum showed one inmate a booklet of prisoners' statements on prison conditions, as well as a leaflet issued by the parents of prisoners from the Golan Heights. The security officer of the prison then entered the room and interrupted the interview. Mr. Fahum was detained for three and a half hours and investigated by the Ashkelon police on suspicion of inciting prisoners to riot. After the intervention of the head of the Israeli Bar Association, Mr. Fahum was released.

Mr. Fahum visited several other prisons after this incident before the denial of access on January 19, 1993. After writing letters of protest, Mr. Fahum and the HRA filed a High Court appeal against the Prison Services and the Ministry of Justice on March 28, 1993. After filing the appeal, Mr. Fahum received word that the injunction had been canceled. He was also advised by the Ministry of Justice and the Prison Services that his appeal should be withdrawn since it was no longer relevant.

LIBYA

MANSUR RASHEED KIKHIA — ABDUCTED

LAWYER-TO-LAWYER NETWORK
APPEAL, DECEMBER 1993

Mansur Rasheed Kikhia, a prominent Libyan lawyer living in the United States, was abducted from his hotel room in Cairo on December 10, 1993, apparently by Libyan government agents. Mr. Kikhia was in Egypt to attend a conference of the Arab Organization of Human Rights, of which he is a founder and board member. Immediately following his disappearance, Reuters reported that

Libyan authorities had vowed to "crush exiled opponents of [President Muammar al-] Gaddafi;" Mansur Kikhia's name was reported to have been mentioned as one who "plotted against the Libyan people." In a speech in November 1992, President Gaddafi told the General People's Congress that the legal profession was "useless," and that, "We do not need professions that do not produce anything."

Mansur Kikhia served as Foreign Minister of Libya from 1972-1973 and as Libya's Permanent Representative to the United Nations between 1975 and 1980, when he resigned in protest against his government's repression and killing of its political opponents at home and abroad. At the time of his abduction, he was serving as the Secretary General of the Libyan National Alliance, a major opposition group.

A number of Libyan lawyers also remain in long-term detention without public charge or trial. The Lawyers Committee is aware of at least three such cases:

JUM'A HASSAN AL-JAZWI	Detained 1981 or 1982, apparently on suspicion of opposition to the government; believed to be held in Abu Salim prison in Tripoli.
RASHID ABDAL-HAMID AL-URFIA	Arrested in Benghazi in February 1982 and accused of being a leader of an illegal opposition group; also detained in Abu Salim prison.

WANIS ASH-SHAREF AL-WARFALI

Arrested in Benghazi on April 23, 1990, apparently for alleged support of a proscribed Islamist opposition group; current whereabouts unknown.

SAUDI ARABIA

COMMITTEE FOR THE DEFENSE OF LEGITIMATE RIGHTS BANNED

On May 13, 1993, the Saudi government shut down the Committee for the Defense of Legitimate Rights (CDLR), a human rights group established by a group of lawyers and professors just ten days earlier. The CDLR was Saudi Arabia's first ever publicly declared human rights group. Several founders of the committee were fired from their government posts or had their law offices closed in reprisal. Hundreds of other CDLR members and sympathizers were detained. Others were barred from leaving the country.

SULEIMAN BIN-ABDULLAH AL-RUSHUDI DETAINED, LICENSE SUSPENDED

In May 1993, the office of Suleiman Al-Rushudi, a lawyer and founding member of the CDLR, was closed down and his license to practice law suspended. On August 8, Mr. Al-Rushudi was arrested at his home in Riyadh. Saudi authorities also searched several houses belonging to Mr. Al-Rushudi and confiscated his personal papers, books and correspondence. He was held incommunicado at an unknown location until his release in late September or early October. He was never charged or brought to trial.

DR. AHMAD BIN 'UTHMAN AT-TUWAIJRI DETAINED

Dr. Ahmad Bin 'Uthman at-Tuwaijri, a 38-year-old lawyer and former Dean of the Department of Education at King Saud University, was detained on 30 August 1993, reportedly for his support of the aims of the CDLR. At the time of his detention, Dr. at-Tuweijiri was completing a book on "the Islamic Constitutional State." He was held incommunicado and reportedly subjected to psychological torture, until his release in late September or early October. Like Mr. Al-Rushudi, he was never charged or brought to trial.

ABDULLAH AL-MASAARI LICENSE SUSPENDED

Lawyer Abdullah al-Masaari was chairman of the CDLR. In May 1993, the Saudi government closed his law office and suspended his license to practice law.

ABDULLAH BIN HAMOUD AT-TUWAIJRI DISMISSED

Abdullah bin at-Tuwaijri, a Professor of Islamic Law, was also a founding member of the CDLR. In May 1993, he was fired from his government teaching post.

Dr. ABD AL-ASIS AL-WUHAIBI DETAINED

Dr. Abd al-Asis al-Wuhaibi is a professor of Islamic law at the al-Imam University. He was arrested in the southern town of Abha while on vacation in August 1993, apparently to punish him for his association with the CDLR. He was released without charge in September.

ABDALLAH BIN ABDEL-RAHMAN AL-JIBBARIN DISMISSED

Abdallah bin Abdel-Rahman al-Jibbarin, a jurist, was dismissed from the government-funded General Directorate of Religious Research. His dismissal was part of the crackdown associated with the banning of the CDLR.

SYRIA

Syria has been under martial law since 1963, and it is the norm for opponents and critics of the regime to be detained indefinitely without charge or trial. Information about the situation of political prisoners is difficult to obtain, since such cases are not publicized by the authorities and access to political prisoners is strictly controlled. However, the 1992 edition of *In Defense of Rights* reported details of nineteen cases of Syrian lawyers in long-term detention. To the best of our knowledge, only one of these lawyers, Muhammad Munir Misouti, was released during 1993. Another, Shakour Tabban, died in prison in November 1992, reportedly as the result of torture and ill-treatment. The other seventeen reportedly remain in detention. They are:

AHMAD AYYASH	Arrested 1982; place of detention unknown.
NAJIB DADAM	Arrested May 1983; reportedly detained in Damascus.
MUHAMMED DAQQO	Arrested 1986; place of detention unknown.
NAIF AL-HAMAWI	Former Attorney General. Arrested January 16, 1991; place of detention unknown.
'ABD AL-KARIM MUHAMMAD HAMOUD	Arrested October 7, 1987; believed to be detained in Sydnaya prison.
ABDALLAH KABBARA	Arrested April 14, 1987; reportedly detained in Aleppo prison.
PHILIPPE KHALAF	Arrested 1981; place of detention unknown.
AFIF JAMIL MEZHER and AKTHAM NU'AYSA	Members of the banned Committee for the Defense of Democratic Freedoms and Human Rights in Syria (CDF); both sentenced to nine years imprisonment with hard labor by a State Security Court in March 1992; in March 1993, Mr. Nu'Aysa undertook a hunger

strike in Sydnaya prison to protest the arbitrary detention of members of the CDF.

WALID MOUTEIRAN — Arrested January 1991; place of detention unknown.

DARWISH AL-RUMI — Arrested 1986; believed to be detained in Damascus.

YUSUF AL-SA'ID — Arrested 1982; place of detention unknown.

DA'OUD SHEHADI — Arrested January 1991; place of detention unknown.

NASH'AT TU'MA — Arrested February 1988; reportedly detained in Sydnaya prison.

RIAD AL-TURK — Arrested October 28, 1980; held incommunicado in solitary confinement at Military Interrogation Branch, Damascus.

MAHMOUD KHALIL YOUNIS — Arrested December 15, 1987; reportedly detained in Sydnaya prison.

MUHAMMAD ZLAYKHA — Arrested November 1987; detained in Latakia military prison.

The Committee for the Defense of Democratic Freedoms and Human Rights (CDF) has also reported that three Lebanese attorneys are currently in detention in Syria without trial. No additional details are available. The three are:

HASSAN BIAN From Ba'albak; arrested January 10, 1992.

NEHMEH JEMAAT From southern Lebanon; arrested October 1991.

FOUAD MOUSSA From Beirut; arrested 1989.

TUNISIA

BECHIR ESSID HARASSED, TRAVEL DENIED

LAWYER-TO-LAWYER NETWORK
APPEAL, JUNE-JULY 1993

Lawyer and political activist Bechir Essid has had his passport withheld by the Tunisian authorities since December 1992 and is denied permission to travel outside the country. The police have kept a close watch on his residence, his office and his clients. They have also used interrogation and harassment to force Mr. Essid's clients to renounce him as their counsel. Mr. Essid was convicted of several offenses related to his involvement in the banned opposition *Rassemblement Unioniste Démocratique* (Democratic Unionist

Assembly) and served over two years in prison until he received a presidential pardon in December 1992.

RADHIA NASROUI HARASSED, THREATENED

Radhia Nasroui, one of the most active Tunisian lawyers in the defense of prisoners accused of political offenses, has been subjected to increasing police harassment. In April 1993, police officers conducted an unauthorized night search of her Tunis home. Maître Nasroui has also been subjected to heavy police surveillance. Prior to her scheduled appearances in court in political trials, it has become routine for her to receive late-night telephone calls from the authorities. In addition she has been interrogated by telephone about her activities with the Tunisian League for Human Rights, of which she is an active member. Maître Nasroui and her family have received anonymous telephone threats, her car was stolen from a guarded lot and a recently hired law clerk was apparently pressured into leaving.

Lawyer to Lawyer Network

THE LAWYER-TO-LAWYER NETWORK IN 1993

Every day lawyers around the world put themselves at personal risk defending the rule of law. Hundreds of these lawyers pay a price for their legal advocacy. Some are harassed, others detained. Each year, a startling number of lawyers and judges are physically attacked and even killed for carrying out their professional duties. When these violations occur the Lawyers Committee activates its Lawyer-to-Lawyer Network. Each month, the Network circulates descriptions of specific cases involving lawyers and judges who have been threatened, harassed or persecuted for their human rights or professional activities. These case summaries are sent to almost 9,000 lawyers, judges, law professors, law students, bar associations and other legal groups. Each member of the Network is asked to write letters to offending governments challenging their actions.

Our efforts can make and have made a difference. In January 1993 Malawian lawyer Vera Chirwa was released from prison (October 1987 Lawyer-to-Lawyer Network Appeal, December 1989 Action Update, May 1992 Action Update, October 1992 Action Update). Florence Simfukwe, daughter of Ms. Chirwa, said that, "Without the persistent efforts of the participants of the Lawyer-to-Lawyer Network I don't believe my mother would have ever been released." In 1993, Network members received replies from the governments of Algeria, Colombia, Mexico, Trinidad and Tobago, Tunisia, Turkey and Uganda.

The effectiveness of the Network is directly tied to the number of lawyers we mobilize in the United States and to our capacity to reach more lawyers and bar groups around the world. This year, financial contributions to the Network allowed us to underwrite the translations of our monthly case descriptions into Arabic. As a result, we have increased participation by Arabic speaking lawyers by 95%. Similarly, in early 1993, we began an expansion initiative in Japan. Last year we only had three Japanese Network members; today, we have nearly 100. In Japan a small advisory group was formed, materials about the Network were translated into Japanese and presentations were made to law firms and bar groups about the work of the Lawyers Committee and the Lawyer-to-Lawyer Network. By the end of 1994, it is anticipated that a permanent translation panel will be in place which will insure the translation of all monthly case descriptions into Japanese. We anticipate that this year's expansion in Japan will serve as a model for future international expansion initiatives.

Network participants continue to recruit new members by asking their colleagues to join. Members of the Network have written articles in bar journals, or hosted small events to promote the work of the Lawyers Committee and the Lawyer-to-Lawyer Network. In an attempt to reach even more lawyers, the Network's monthly case descriptions are now available on Peacenet.

Looking forward, we will continue to explore ways to communicate more effectively with members to enable us to respond more quickly, and in effect, better protect our colleagues at risk. We will continue to rely on information supplied to us by our many members regarding potential cases for our monthly Network Appeals as well as on suggestions for recruitment initiatives and additional ways that we may become more effective.

Jéneen M. Masih
Coordinator,
Lawyer-to-Lawyer Network

1993 Lawyer-to-Lawyer Network Cases

January:	María Teresa Jardí, Mexico Henry Kayondo, Uganda Francis Sama, Cameroon (Update) Ophelia Senze, Cameroon (Update) Rafael Efraín Ortiz, Dominican Republic (Update) Paul Yves Joseph, Haiti (Update) Vera Chirwa, Malawi (Update)
February:	Brahim Taouti, Algeria Ali Zouita, Algeria Association of Democratic Lawyers (ADL), Peru
March:	Kulwant Singh Saini, India Metin Can, Turkey José Eduardo Pineda Valenzuela, El Salvador (Update) María Teresa Jardí, Mexico (Update)
April:	Brahim Taouti, Algeria (Action Update) Héctor Hugo Pérez Aguilera, Guatemala Mario Guillermo Ruíz Wong, Guatemala Mario René Díaz López, Guatemala
May:	Eduardo Umaña Mendoza, Colombia Abdullah al-Maasari, Saudi Arabia Suleiman bin-Abdullah al-Rushudi, Saudi Arabia Abdullah bin-Hamoud Tuwaijri, Saudi Arabia Héctor Hugo Pérez Aguilera, Guatemala (Action Update)

	Mario Guillermo Ruiz Wong, Guatemala (Action Update)
	Mario René Diaz López, Guatemala (Action Update)
	Fevzi Veznedaroglu, Turkey (Update)
	Henry Kayondo, Uganda (Update)
	Leonid Kurgansky, Ukraine (Update)
	Dumisa Buhle Ntsebeza, South Africa (Update)
June/July:	Femi Falana, Nigeria
	Chief Gani Fawehinmi, Nigeria
	Bechir Essid, Tunisia
	Fevzi Veznedaroglu, Turkey (Action Update)
October:	Yu Haocheng, China
	Guy Malary, Haiti
	Reginald Armour, Trinidad and Tobago
	Gregory Dalzin, Trinidad and Tobago
	Christopher Hamel-Smith, Trinidad and Tobago
	Douglas Mendez, Trinidad and Tobago
November:	Rafael Barrios Mendivil and members of the *Corporación Colectivo de Abogados*, Colombia
	Fatlik Lila, Kosovo
	Sokol Dobruna, Kosovo
	Reginald Armour, Trinidad and Tobago (Update)
	Gregory Dalzin, Trinidad and Tobago (Update)

Christopher Hamel-Smith, Trinidad and Tobago (Update)
Douglas Mendez, Trinidad and Tobago (Update)
Femi Falana, Nigeria (Update)
Chief Gani Fawehinmi, Nigeria (Update)
Beko Ransome-Kuti, Nigeria (Update)

December: Mansur Rasheed Kikhia, Libya

APPENDICES

Basic Principles on the Independence of the Judiciary*

Whereas in the Charter of the United Nations the peoples of the world affirm, *inter alia,* their determination to establish conditions under which justice can be maintained to achieve international cooperation in promoting and encouraging respect for human rights and fundamental freedoms without any discrimination,

Whereas the Universal Declaration of Human Rights enshrines in particular the principles of equality before the law, of the presumption of innocence and of the right to a fair and public hearing by a competent, independent and impartial tribunal established by law,

Whereas the organization and administration of justice in every country should be inspired by those principles, and efforts should be undertaken to translate them fully into reality,

Whereas rules concerning the exercise of judicial office should aim at enabling judges to act in accordance with those principles,

Whereas judges are charged with the ultimate decision over life, freedom, rights, duties and property of citizens,

Whereas the Sixth United Nations Congress on the Prevention of Crime and the Treatment of Offenders, by its resolution 16, called upon the Committee on Crime Prevention and Control to include among its priorities the elaboration of guidelines relating to the

*Adopted by the Seventh United Nations Congress on the Prevention of Crime and the Treatment of Offenders, held in Milan, Italy in August and September 1985, and welcomed by the 40th General Assembly of the United Nations in resolution 40/146, adopted December 13, 1985.

independence of judges and the selection, professional training and status of judges and prosecutors,

Whereas it is, therefore, appropriate that consideration be first given to the role of judges in relation to the system of justice and to the importance of their selection, training and conduct,

The following basic principles, formulated to assist Member States in their task of securing and promoting the independence of the judiciary should be taken into account and respected by Governments within the framework of their national legislation and practice and be brought to the attention of judges, lawyers, members of the executive and the legislature and the public in general. The principles have been formulated principally with professional judges in mind, but they apply equally, as appropriate, to lay judges, where they exist.

Independence of the judiciary

1. The independence of the judiciary shall be guaranteed by the State and enshrined in the Constitution or the law of the country. It is the duty of all governmental and other institutions to respect and observe the independence of the judiciary.

2. The judiciary shall decide matters before them impartially, on the basis of facts and in accordance with the law, without any restrictions, improper influences, inducements, pressures, threats or interferences, direct or indirect, from any quarter or for any reason.

3. The judiciary shall have jurisdiction over all issues of a judicial nature and shall have exclusive authority to decide whether an

issue submitted for its decision is within its competence as defined by law.

4. There shall not be any inappropriate or unwarranted interference with the judicial process, nor shall judicial decisions by the courts be subject to revision. This principle is without prejudice to judicial review or to mitigation or commutation by competent authorities of sentences imposed by the judiciary, in accordance with the law.

5. Everyone shall have the right to be tried by ordinary courts or tribunals using established legal procedures. Tribunals that do not use the duly established procedures of the legal process shall not be created to displace the jurisdiction belonging to the ordinary courts or judicial tribunals.

6. The principle of the independence of the judiciary entitles and requires the judiciary to ensure that judicial proceedings are conducted fairly and that the rights of the parties are respected.

7. It is the duty of each Member State to provide adequate resources to enable the judiciary to properly perform its functions.

Freedom of expression and association

8. In accordance with the Universal Declaration of Human Rights, members of the judiciary are like other citizens entitled to freedom of expression, belief, association and assembly; provided, however, that in exercising such rights, judges shall always conduct themselves in such a manner as to preserve the dignity of their office and the impartiality and independence of the judiciary.

9. Judges shall be free to form and join associations of judges or other organizations to represent their interests, to promote their professional training and to protect their judicial independence.

Qualifications, selections and training

10. Persons selected for judicial office shall be individuals of integrity and ability with appropriate training or qualifications in law. Any method of judicial selection shall safeguard against judicial appointments for improper motives. In the selection of judges, there shall be no discrimination against a person on the grounds of race, colour, sex, religion, political or other opinion, national or social origin, property, birth or status, except that a requirement, that a candidate for judicial office must be a national of the country concerned, shall not be considered discriminatory.

Conditions of service and tenure

11. The term of office of judges, their independence, security, adequate remuneration, conditions of service, pensions and the age of retirement shall be adequately secured by law.

12. Judges, whether appointed or elected, shall have guaranteed tenure until a mandatory retirement age or the expiry of their term of office, where such exists.

13. Promotion of judges, wherever such a system exists, should be based on objective factors, in particular ability, integrity and experience.

14. The assignment of cases to judges within the court to which they belong is an internal matter of judicial administration.

Professional secrecy and immunity

15. The judiciary shall be bound by professional secrecy with regard to their deliberations and to confidential information acquired in the course of their duties other than in public proceedings, and shall not be compelled to testify on such matters.

16. Without prejudice to any disciplinary procedure or to any right of appeal or to compensation from the State, in accordance with national law, judges should enjoy personal immunity from civil suits for monetary damages for improper acts or omissions in the exercise of their judicial functions.

Discipline, suspension and removal

17. A charge or complaint made against a judge in his/her judicial and professional capacity shall be processed expeditiously and fairly under an appropriate procedure. The judge shall have the right to a fair hearing. The examination of the matter at its initial stage shall be kept confidential, unless otherwise requested by the judge.

18. Judges shall be subject to suspension or removal only for reasons of incapacity or behaviour that renders them unfit to discharge their duties.

19. All disciplinary, suspension or removal proceedings shall be determined in accordance with established standards of judicial conduct.

20. Decisions in disciplinary, suspension or removal proceedings should be subject to an independent review. This principle may not apply to the decisions of the highest court and those of the legislature in impeachment or similar proceedings.

Basic Principles on the Role of Lawyers**

Whereas in the Charter of the United Nations the peoples of the world affirm, *inter alia*, their determination to establish conditions under which justice can be maintained, and proclaim as one of their purposes the achievement of international co-operation in promoting and encouraging respect for human rights and fundamental freedoms without distinction as to race, sex, language, or religion,

Whereas the Universal Declaration of Human Rights enshrines the principles of equality before law, the presumption of innocence, the right to a fair and public hearing by an independent and impartial tribunal, and all the guarantees necessary for the defence of everyone charged with a penal offence,

Whereas the International Covenant on Civil and Political Rights proclaims, in addition, the right to be tried without undue delay and the right to a fair and public hearing by a competent, independent and impartial tribunal established by law,

Whereas the International Covenant on Economic, Social and Cultural Rights recalls the obligation of States under the Charter to promote universal respect for, and observance of, human rights and freedoms,

---

**Adopted by the Eighth United Nations Congress on the Prevention of Crime and the Treatment of Offenders, held in Havana, Cuba in August and September 1990, and welcomed by the 45th General Assembly of the United Nations in resolution 45/121, adopted December 14, 1990.

Whereas the Body of Principles for the Protection of All Persons under Any Form of Detention or Imprisonment provides that a detained person shall be entitled to have the assistance of, and to communicate and consult with, legal counsel,

Whereas the Standard Minimum Rules for the Treatment of Prisoners recommend, in particular, that legal assistance and confidential communication with counsel should be ensured to untried prisoners,

Whereas the safeguards guaranteeing protection of those facing the death penalty reaffirm the right of everyone suspected or charged with a crime for which capital punishment may be imposed to adequate legal assistance at all stages of the proceedings, in accordance with article 14 of the International Covenant on Civil and Political Rights,

Whereas the Declaration of Basic Principles of Justice for Victims of Crime and Abuse of Power recommends measures to be taken at the international and national levels to improve access to justice and fair treatment, restitution, compensation and assistance for victims of crime,

Whereas adequate protection of the human rights and fundamental freedoms to which all persons are entitled, be they economic, social and cultural, or civil and political, requires that all persons have effective access to legal services provided by an independent legal profession,

Whereas professional associations of lawyers have a vital role to play in upholding professional standards and ethics, protecting their members from persecution and improper restrictions and infringements, providing legal services to all in need of them, and co-operating with governmental and other institutions in furthering the ends of justice and public interest,

The Basic Principles on the Role of Lawyers, set forth below, which have been formulated to assist Member States in their task of promoting and ensuring the proper role of lawyers, should be respected and taken into account by Governments within the framework of their national legislation and practice and should be brought to the attention of lawyers as well as other persons, such as judges, prosecutors, members of the executive and the legislature, and the public in general. These principles shall also apply, as appropriate, to persons who exercise the functions of lawyers without having the formal status of lawyers.

Access to lawyers and legal services

1. All persons are entitled to call upon the assistance of a lawyer of their choice to protect and establish their rights and to defend them in all stages of criminal proceedings.

2. Governments shall ensure that efficient procedures and responsive mechanisms for effective and equal access to lawyers are provided for all persons within their territory and subject to their jurisdiction, without distinction of any kind, such as discrimination based on race, colour, ethnic origin, sex, language, religion, political or other opinion, national or social origin, property, birth, economic or other status.

3. Governments shall ensure the provision of sufficient funding and other resources for legal services to the poor and, as necessary, to other disadvantaged persons. Professional associations of lawyers shall co-operate in the organization and provision of services, facilities and other resources.

4. Governments and professional associations of lawyers shall promote programmes to inform the public about their rights and duties under the law and the important role of lawyers in protecting their fundamental freedoms. Special attention should be given to assisting the poor and other disadvantaged persons so as to enable them to assert their rights and where necessary call upon the assistance of lawyers.

Special safeguards in criminal justice matters

5. Governments shall ensure that all persons are immediately informed by the competent authority of their right to be assisted by a lawyer of their own choice upon arrest or detention or when charged with a criminal offence.

6. Any such persons who do not have a lawyer shall, in all cases in which the interests of justice so require, be entitled to have a lawyer of experience and competence commensurate with the nature of the offence assigned to them in order to provide effective legal assistance, without payment by them if they lack sufficient means to pay for such services.

7. Governments shall further ensure that all persons arrested or detained, with or without criminal charge, shall have prompt access to

a lawyer, and in any case not later than forty-eight hours from the time of arrest or detention.

8. All arrested, detained or imprisoned persons shall be provided with adequate opportunities, time and facilities to be visited by and to communicate and consult with a lawyer, without delay, interception or censorship and in full confidentiality. Such consultations may be within sight, but not within hearing, of law enforcement officials.

Qualifications and training

9. Governments, professional associations of lawyers and educational institutions shall ensure that lawyers have appropriate education and training and be made aware of the ideals and ethical duties of the lawyer and of human rights and fundamental freedoms recognized by national and international law.

10. Governments, professional associations of lawyers and educational institutions shall ensure that there is no discrimination against a person with respect to entry into or continued practice within the legal profession on the grounds of race, colour, sex, ethnic origin, religion, political or other opinion, national or social origin, property, birth, economic or other status, except that a requirement, that a lawyer must be a national of the country concerned, shall not be considered discriminatory.

11. In countries where there exist groups, communities or regions whose needs for legal services are not met, particularly where such groups have distinct cultures, traditions or languages or have been the victims of past discrimination, Governments, professional associations of lawyers and educational institutions should take special measures

to provide opportunities for candidates from these groups to enter the legal profession and should ensure that they receive training appropriate to the needs of their groups.

Duties and responsibilities

12. Lawyers shall at all times maintain the honour and dignity of their profession as essential agents of the administration of justice.

13. The duties of lawyers towards their clients shall include:

a) Advising clients as to their legal rights and obligations, and as to the working of the legal system in so far as it is relevant to the legal rights and obligations of the clients;
b) Assisting clients in every appropriate way, and taking legal action to protect their interests;
c) Assisting clients before courts, tribunals or administrative authorities, where appropriate.

14. Lawyers, in protecting the rights of their clients and in promoting the cause of justice, shall seek to uphold human rights and fundamental freedoms recognized by national and international law and shall at all times act freely and diligently in accordance with the law and recognized standards and ethics of the legal profession.

15. Lawyers shall always loyally respect the interests of their clients.

Guarantees for the functioning of lawyers

16. Governments shall ensure that lawyers a) are able to perform all of their professional functions without intimidation, hindrance,

harassment or improper interference; b) are able to travel and to consult with their clients freely both within their own country and abroad; and c) shall not suffer, or be threatened with, prosecution or administrative, economic or other sanctions for any action taken in accordance with recognized professional duties, standards and ethics.

17. Where the security of lawyers is threatened as a result of discharging their functions, they shall be adequately safeguarded by the authorities.

18. Lawyers shall not be identified with their clients or their clients' causes as a result of discharging their functions.

19. No court or administrative authority before whom the right to counsel is recognized shall refuse to recognize the right of a lawyer to appear before it for his or her client unless that lawyer has been disqualified in accordance with national law and practice and in conformity with these principles.

20. Lawyers shall enjoy civil and penal immunity for relevant statements made in good faith in written or oral pleadings or in their professional appearances before a court, tribunal or other legal or administrative authority.

21. It is the duty of the competent authorities to ensure lawyers access to appropriate information, files and documents in their possession or control in sufficient time to enable lawyers to provide effective legal assistance to their clients. Such access should be provided at the earliest appropriate time.

22. Governments shall recognize and respect that all communications and consultations between lawyers and their clients within their professional relationship are confidential.

Freedom of expression and association

23. Lawyers like other citizens are entitled to freedom of expression, belief, association and assembly. In particular, they shall have the right to take part in public discussion of matters concerning the law, the administration of justice and the promotion and protection of human rights and to join or form local, national or international organizations and attend their meetings, without suffering professional restrictions by reason of their lawful action or their membership in a lawful organization. In exercising these rights, lawyers shall always conduct themselves in accordance with the law and the recognized standards and ethics of the legal profession.

Professional associations of lawyers

24. Lawyers shall be entitled to form and join self-governing professional associations to represent their interests, promote their continuing education and training and protect their professional integrity. The executive body of the professional associations shall be elected by its members and shall exercise its functions without external interference.

25. Professional associations of lawyers shall co-operate with Governments to ensure that everyone has effective and equal access to legal services and that lawyers are able, without improper interference, to counsel and assist their clients in accordance with the law and recognized professional standards and ethics.

Disciplinary proceedings

26. Codes of professional conduct for lawyers shall be established by the legal profession through its appropriate organs, or by legislation, in accordance with national law and custom and recognized international standards and norms.

27. Charges or complaints made against lawyers in their professional capacity shall be processed expeditiously and fairly under appropriate procedures. Lawyers shall have the right to a fair hearing, including the right to be assisted by a lawyer of their choice.

28. Disciplinary proceedings against lawyers shall be brought before an impartial disciplinary committee established by the legal profession, before an independent statutory authority, or before a court, and shall be subject to an independent judicial review.

29. All disciplinary proceedings shall be determined in accordance with the code of professional conduct and other recognized standards and ethics of the legal profession and in the light of these principles.

LAWYERS COMMITTEE FOR HUMAN RIGHTS STAFF

MICHAEL H. POSNER
Executive Director

ADOTEI AKWEI, Africa
PATRICIA ARMSTRONG, IFI Liaison
JOHN ASSADI, Staff Attorney, part-time
GEORGE BLACK, Research and Editorial Director
LILI BROWN, Development Director
LISA A. BROWN, Administrative Assistant, Finance & Personnel
WALTER BURRIER, Staff Attorney, part-time
JEFFREY CHASE, Staff Attorney, part-time
TINA M. CHRISTOPULOS, Program Assistant
SANDRA M. COLE, Finance & Personnel
MARTHA LYN DOGGETT, Latin America & the Caribbean
JOSEPH T. ELDRIDGE, Director, Washington Office
ERIC HACKWORTH, Office Services
NEIL HICKS, Middle East/North Africa
ANNE HOYT, Development Coordinator
HELEN KAPSTEIN, Legal Assistant
MARIANA KATZAROVA, Europe
JANICE CURRERI, Administrative Assistant
VIRGINIA PETERS MANN, Executive Assistant
ANNE-MARIE MARABLE, Administrative Assistant, Witness
STEPHANIE MARKS, Asylum Representation Program
JENEEN M. MASIH, Lawyer-to-Lawyer Network
ELISA C. MASSIMINO, Staff Attorney, Washington Office
ANNETTE O'DONNELL, Executive Assistant
SARAH H. PAOLETTI, Office Administrator, Washington Office
COURTNAY PETERS, Program Assistant
LISA Z. PILGRIM, Foundation Coordinator
DEBORAH STEWART, Reception
ROBERT O. WEINER, Latin America & the Caribbean
WALTER WEISS, Staff Attorney, part-time
CANDY WHITTOME, IGO/NGO Liaison